Praise for

LONGEVITY FOR DOGS

"As the guy who started the biohacking movement for humans, I'm so excited about Dr. Richter's book, Longevity for Dogs. *Of course, we can also use biohacking to improve—and extend—the lives of our furry companions. In his book, Dr. Richter shares his vast knowledge and expertise on pet nutrition, exercise, and environmental enrichment. The strategies he outlines are not only effective, but they're also practical and easy to implement. So, if you're a pet owner who's interested in giving your furry friend the best possible life, then I highly recommend checking out* Longevity for Dogs *by Dr. Richter. Your pets will thank you for it!"*

— **Dave Asprey**, father of biohacking, four-time *New York Times* best-selling author, host of *The Human Upgrade Podcast,* CEO of Upgrade Labs

"We all want to live longer healthier lives, but if we were realistic, we'd like the same and more for our dogs! Well, now you can! Dr. Richter, using much of the same knowledge, supplements, and eating tricks that I speak about for human longevity, has applied this to our canine companions and it's all here in this book! Now we can all grow old (younger?) together for longer and better!"

— **Steven R. Gundry, M.D.**, multiple *New York Times* best-selling author of *The Plant Paradox* series and founder of GundryMD.com

"I have personally experienced how Dr. Gary Richter's approach to pet care has enhanced the longevity and vitality of my fur babies, and I am forever grateful! His new book, Longevity for Dogs, *empowers pet parents through science-backed nutrition, supplementation, exercise, and lifestyle recommendations to help their four-legged family members live long and happy lives. I highly recommend this book as a resource and look forward to a fast-approaching world where humans and pets are aging well, together."*

— **Serena Poon, C.N., C.H.C., C.H.N.**, CEO and founder of Serena Loves LLC and Just Add Water; co-founder of Fully Aligned Co LLC

"Gary Richter is a gift to the veterinary world. He understands not only pet health but has now elegantly translated insights from human longevity medicine into the pet world with clarity and practicality. If you want more great years with your dog, you'll love this book!"

— **Jeffrey Gladden, M.D., F.A.C.C.**, founder and CEO of Gladden Longevity

"If you love your dog then you need this book. Death comes too soon to our four-legged friends, but now it doesn't have to. Dr. Richter has written a groundbreaking book providing a step-by-step guide to giving your loving companion not only more years but also a higher quality of life. Dr. Richter is a thoughtful, kind, and brilliant medical professional who is a veterinary's vet that everybody wishes they had as their own personal physician. His book Longevity for Dogs *provides not only a clear explanation of the science of longevity but is also a practical guide to the steps you can take now to ensure your pets will have the longest, healthiest life possible. Buy this book for your best friend. Buy this book for yourself, because keeping your best friend healthy helps keep you healthy."*

— **Dr. Gary Kaplan**, medical director, Kaplan Center for Integrative Medicine, Mclean, Virginia, clinical associate professor, Georgetown University School of Medicine, author of *Why You Are Still Sick: How Infections Can Break Your Immune System and How You Can Recover*

"Dr. Richter is one the leading experts on pet health, biohacking, and nutrition. This book is a groundbreaking resource that's taking tough (and brilliant) concepts and making them super simple."

— **Shawn Wells, M.P.H., R.D., L.D.N., C.I.S.S.N.**, biochemist, formulator, and international best-selling author of *The ENERGY Formula*

"We are on the threshold of a whole new age of how medical science views and upholds proper healthcare and longevity. This book nails it on the head. While being extremely comprehensive, Dr. Richter has kept a potentially boring and confusing subject easy to understand, while being a fascinating and enjoyable read. He welcomes us to the necessary future of medicine and healthcare for our companion animals and even us too."

— **Marty Goldstein, D.V.M.**, author of *The Nature of Animal Healing* and *The Spirit of Animal Healing*

LONGEVITY FOR DOGS

ALSO BY GARY RICHTER, M.S., D.V.M., C.V.C., C.V.A.

The Ultimate Pet Health Guide: Breakthrough Nutrition and Integrative Care for Dogs and Cats

Longevity for Cats: A Holistic, Individualized Approach to Helping Your Feline Friend Live Longer—and Healthier

Please visit:

Hay House USA: www.hayhouse.com®
Hay House Australia: www.hayhouse.com.au
Hay House UK: www.hayhouse.co.uk
Hay House India: www.hayhouse.co.in

LONGEVITY FOR DOGS

A HOLISTIC, INDIVIDUALIZED APPROACH TO HELPING YOUR CANINE COMPANION LIVE LONGER—AND HEALTHIER

GARY RICHTER, M.S., D.V.M.

HAY HOUSE INDIA
New Delhi • London • Sydney
Carlsbad, California • New York City

Published in India by: Hay House Publishers India: www.hayhouse.co.in
Published in the United States by: Hay House, Inc.: www.hayhouse.com®
Published in Australia by: Hay House Australia Pty. Ltd.: www.hay house.com.au
Published in the United Kingdom by: Hay House UK, Ltd.: www.hayhouse.co.uk

Project editor: Nicolette Salamanca Young • *Indexer:* Shapiro Indexing Services
Cover design: Scott Breidenthal • *Interior design:* Karim J. Garcia

First Hay House India Edition 2024

ISBN: 978-81-19554-60-7

Printed at Repro India Limited

CONTENTS

This book is dedicated to every animal who has shown me how to be a better healer and how to love unconditionally.

INTRODUCTION

Our dogs should live forever—or at least as long as we do. This sentiment is shared by pretty much every dog parent who comes into my office. The reality, of course, is dog ownership (or guardianship, if you prefer) is filled with years of loving and unforgettable experiences that end with devastating loss.

The death of a beloved dog is literally a life-altering event. For many, the loss of a canine family member can be more impactful than the loss of a human family member. After all, we don't receive unconditional love from the humans in our life, and for those of us who aren't perfect (all of us), having a companion who forgives and forgets is a gift beyond measure. In my 25 years of practicing veterinary medicine, I have held hands with, hugged, and counseled scores of dog owners, with discussions about smooth transitions, quality of life, and how allowing our family member to have a peaceful and painless passing is the last, best favor we can do for them.

It's all true. Euthanasia as a last treatment option is both incredibly difficult and a wonderful gift. Anyone who has ever seen a family member (human or animal) in pain at the end of life will understand that transitioning before things get really bad is a blessing. But what if there was a way to help our pets live longer and healthier lives and delay those sad, final days by a few—or even many—years? What if there was a way to postpone that day indefinitely?

Longevity science for humans is a rapidly growing field of study that has attracted some of the best and brightest scientific minds. My first real exposure to longevity as an achievable goal began in 2020 with two specific events. The first was a trip to Dallas, where I met Dr. Jeffrey Gladden, an interventional cardiologist by training who has now turned his sights on improving the longevity and performance of his patients. Sitting down with Dr. Gladden and discussing what we know about longevity and how we can affect the multiple pathways in the body that impact aging brought into focus that longevity is now much more than a general concept. I realized that through diagnostic testing, diet, and the use of supplements—and sometimes pharmaceuticals and medical treatments—we can slow and frequently even reverse the ticking clock in our bodies.

The second revelation occurred with an unexpected phone call. My good friend Richard Rossi is the creator of an event called the Congress of Future Medical Leaders, which brings together thousands of high-achieving high school students who have professional aspirations in medicine. Top doctors, scientists, and even Nobel Prize winners regularly present at this meeting. I have been blessed with being a speaker and have had the opportunity to shine a light on both veterinary medicine and holistic/integrative medicine for these future medical professionals. Richard's skill at creating and hosting an event is the best I have ever seen. When he called in 2020 to tell me he was assembling a small group of people to have in-depth discussions about longevity science, well, let's just say he "had me at hello."

As I write this, there have since been four meetings of the group, called DaVinci 50, and it has been an eye-opening experience. The group, capped at 50 participants, allows for up-close and personal discussions with the speakers and the other brilliant minds in the room. Some of the world's greatest scientists in longevity research—including David Sinclair, George Church, Aubrey de Grey, Greg Fahy, and more—have presented. The research has been, to say the least, cutting-edge, and I'll cover a lot of it in this book.

By the end of 2020, I was turning my own sights toward longevity medicine for pets. I've been practicing integrative medicine for decades, utilizing both conventional allopathic medicine and acupuncture, herbs, chiropractic hyperbaric oxygen, ozone, and other more holistic methods. I took my first steps down the pathway of integrative medicine because I didn't like telling pet owners that we had exhausted all treatment options, and their only choice was to discuss end-of-life planning. The truth is that there are many beneficial alternative therapies—those outside of medication and surgery—that can be advantageous to our pets. As I learned about and implemented more ways to help my patients, I found that dogs were living longer and better lives than they "should" have, based on what is expected from allopathic medicine alone. During these years practicing integrative medicine, I focused primarily on maintaining quality of life. Increasing quantity of life was an added bonus, but it wasn't until meeting Dr. Gladden and attending DaVinci 50 that I began to look at longevity as an achievable primary goal. Medical science has progressed to the point where we now understand many of the metabolic pathways in the body that affect aging, and through new diagnostic tests, we can gather actionable information to slow the aging process.

My goal in writing this book is to provide you, as your dog's companion and caregiver, with an accessible and actionable guide you can use to help your dog live a longer—and healthier—life. By necessity, we are going to discuss some science, but no Ph.D. or medical degree will be required to successfully read and, hopefully, enjoy this book. We will explore both currently accessible options and the cutting-edge science that will become available for humans and pets in the near future.

We are at an inflection point in science and medicine where the end of life may no longer be inevitable or, at the very least, will be delayed significantly. That may seem like an outrageous claim, but I encourage you to read on! Science is right on the brink of solving aging, and while the vast majority of this research has been focused on people, you and I both know that the lives of our dogs are at least as important as our own silly human lives.

I hope you find this book as informative and enjoyable to read as it has been for me to write. Most important, may the information you find within these pages help you to help your dog(s) live their longest, healthiest life!

PART I

UNDERSTANDING LONGEVITY SCIENCE

CHAPTER 1

WHAT DOES "LONGEVITY" REALLY MEAN?

The average dog's life expectancy is somewhere between 10 and 14 years old. The oldest dog I have ever personally seen was a Chihuahua who passed away at 22, and the oldest recorded in the *Guinness Book of World Records* was 30 years and 8 months old at the time of his death.[1] But what if 30 was not a one-in-many-millions outlier? What if these ages became normal and expected life spans for our best friends? What if there was no time limit on our dogs' life span at all? This is where the modern science of longevity comes in.

When you think of *longevity,* perhaps you imagine living a long and healthy life. Maybe it means you're remembered after you're gone or your family (and genetics) survives for many generations into the future. These are both viable perspectives on longevity, but for the purposes of this book, we are interested in something that has long been sought after by scientists, mystics, and theologians, with no success. At its most basic level, longevity science is about finding solutions that extend life not only to a dramatically advanced age but also potentially indefinitely.

Modern longevity science is a pretty new field, and a lot of the current research has been done in the laboratory on cell cultures or lab animals, ranging from nematodes (worms) to fruit flies to rodents. Most of the diagnostic and treatment strategies we will discuss have been designed for use in humans, although to be clear, they are working with the same lab-animal data we are. From a veterinary-medicine perspective, longevity science is about as new as it comes. Barely anyone in the veterinary profession is even thinking about diagnostics and treatments specifically targeting longevity for dogs, although I promise you that will change in the near future. For now, much of the research, diagnostic testing, and therapies we discuss for your dog are based on what we know from the lab-animal data and what is occurring within the field of longevity medicine for humans. On the occasions where there are dog-specific studies, tests, or treatments, I will be sure to highlight them.

Clearly, we all want our dogs to live more years, but it really has to be about more than just quantity. I can tell you that the 22-year-old Chihuahua who was a patient in my care was not in the best of shape for the last several years of his life. He had poor mobility, had lost most of his eyesight and hearing, and was not cognitively all there. Any of us who has seen what aging can do to the body and mind—whether canine or human—knows that purely living to an advanced age is not always ideal and comes with its own issues. Instead, longevity is about maintaining a high *quality* of life for the entire life span—what is sometimes referred to as *health span*. In other words, while we can't stop the aging process altogether (yet), we can work to avoid the health declines that come with it. My goal (and hopefully yours as well) is for our dogs to live far longer than the 10- to 14-year average *and* to maintain their youth and vigor until the end—increasing both quantity and quality of life.

All too frequently, aging dogs and their people come into my office, and when I ask how the dog is doing, the response is, "She's doing great, just slowing down a little now that she is getting older." Slowing down is an external sign that body systems are beginning to function inefficiently. This may be due to arthritis, back pain, organ disease, cognitive impairment, or any number of other medical diagnoses. But this slowing down is often the first visible sign of a dog's decline. The truth is, once these changes are noticeable, they have been present for quite some time.

When investigating longevity for dogs, we necessarily need to take a hard look at what aging is and what it does. I realize that can be a little difficult, because it is always more comfortable to not seriously consider a furry companion's mortality. But as with any challenge we encounter, the solution here requires an understanding of what went wrong and why. This is how we are going to approach longevity for dogs. My goal as a veterinarian, and yours as a pet owner, is to prevent as many of these things from happening and to slow or reverse those that have already occurred. Modern medicine can already do some of this with things like stem cells and platelet-rich plasma, but where the science is *going* will blow your mind.

The history of humanity's search for a means to ward off death is about as old as human history itself. Over 2,200 years ago, the Chinese emperor Qin Shi Huang charged his subjects with finding a potion to give him eternal life.[2] Qin Shi Huang was certainly not alone in his quest. From the story of the immortal Gilgamesh in 600 B.C. to Ponce de León searching for the fountain of youth in the early 1500s to the cutting edge of modern longevity science, people have not let go of the idea of being able to extend life or completely stave off the inevitability of death. Though magical elixirs and fountains have largely been left in the rearview mirror, the question of longevity hasn't changed. People are still asking how to prolong youth, health, and life. But now, we can start by investigating the root of the problem: What are the processes that lead to physical and mental decline, aging, and ultimately death? In this chapter, I will introduce and explain the 14 hallmarks of aging so that you can begin to focus on how to prevent these processes from occurring in your beloved dog.

THE HALLMARKS OF AGING

Let's begin with an understanding of how aging works. At its core, aging is a loss of function that occurs over time and eventually leads to a body being incapable of maintaining life. This loss of function is due to a complicated web of entangled bodily processes, and the bad news is that there is not, and likely will never be, one magic pill to keep us—and our dogs—young forever. Slowing or halting aging is a multifactorial process that requires addressing many different aspects of health on a cellular level.

One of the most comprehensive descriptions of the mechanics of aging can be found in a 2013 article in the medical journal *Cell*. Titled "The Hallmarks of Aging," it outlines nine specific categories that lead to loss of function, and most of the current research into life extension is directed at affecting one or more of these.[3] The categories sound pretty complicated (scientists tend to favor the complicated), but we'll break down what is crucial to understand. In large part, all the testing and treatment strategies discussed in the upcoming chapters will be focused on addressing one or more of these hallmarks: *genomic instability, telomere attrition, epigenetic alterations, loss of proteostasis, deregulated nutrient sensing, mitochondrial dysfunction, cellular senescence, stem cell exhaustion,* and *altered intercellular communication.*

More recently, at a symposium in Copenhagen in 2022, 5 more hallmarks of aging were introduced, bringing the total to 14: *compromised autophagy, microbiome disturbance, altered mechanical properties, splicing dysregulation,* and *inflammation.*[4] Some of the new categories, such as inflammation, were already described in the original nine but have now been made their own separate category. For the purposes of our longevity discussions, we will focus largely on the original nine hallmarks of aging, as they are the most well studied and provide good options for intervention.

Genomic Instability

The material responsible for all life on Earth is deoxyribonucleic acid, or DNA. To make a very complex story short, DNA is the code that allows living organisms to be what they are, whether plant, animal, bacteria, or fungi. DNA utilizes chemical compounds called *nucleotides* in specific sequences to form *genes,* and genes are the code that dictates what proteins a cell needs to form any one part of the body. We can use the analogy of a book to think about DNA. The nucleotides are the alphabet; although rather than 26 letters, in DNA there are only 4: *A, T, C,* and *G.* These four letters are paired into nucleotide bases, and they have to be strung together in specific ways to form words, or DNA.

When you're reading, each individual word has limited meaning by itself, but when words are put into sentences, and sentences are strung together to form paragraphs, much greater meaning emerges. DNA's sentences and paragraphs are genes. Together, the paragraphs in a book tell a complete story, in much the same way that genes are responsible for making up an organism. The full complement of genes in any organism is referred to as its *genome*.

When cells in any organism need to grow or repair themselves, they undergo a process called mitosis. During mitosis, the DNA in the cell divides and then remakes itself whole so that each new cell is an exact copy of the original. However, that process is not perfect. Even in a healthy body, there is an error in 1 in every approximately 100,000 nucleotides copied. While there are mechanisms in the cell to fix DNA damage, not everything is repairable.

As a body ages, the error rate of DNA replication tends to increase. When these errors begin to pile up, we wind up with dysfunctional or nonfunctional genes. This can lead to cells being unable to create the necessary proteins to maintain health or even to their becoming cancerous. The inability to replicate the genome with high fidelity (accuracy) is known as *genomic instability*.

Aging and other internal processes, however, are not the only causes of genomic instability. External factors can also play a role. Radiation from sources such as X-rays, prolonged sun exposure, and radon are known to cause genomic instability. While the mechanisms are somewhat different for each, the ionizing radiation from these sources causes breaks in DNA that can lead to nonfunctional genes or mutations of genes. Similarly, chemicals such as air and water pollutants (carbon monoxide, lead, particulates, agricultural by-products, and so forth), smoke (cigarette or otherwise), and certain drugs can also lead to genomic instability and altered DNA methylation (which, as will be explained in a subsequent section, is a critical part of *epigenetics*, or which genes get expressed).

Interestingly, research into the genomes of people who are over 100 years old shows that they have an increased ability to repair damaged DNA. Studies are underway to better understand exactly how this works, but it seems clear genetics, diet, and lifestyle all play a role. While there isn't much you or your dog can do about the genes you are born with, diet and lifestyle are factors completely within your control, and we'll take a look at that in Chapters 3 and 4.

Telomere Attrition

Genomic instability is not the only facet of DNA replication that can affect aging. The second hallmark of aging, *telomere attrition*, represents another hurdle standing in the way of your dog's ability to generate new cells when they are needed to maintain optimal health.

Chromosomes are the entirety of the genome. Essentially, they are strands of DNA that are wound up very tightly to make them compact enough to fit in the cell nucleus. Each chromosome is paired, as one copy comes from Mom and one from Dad. Dogs have 78 chromosomes (39 pairs). For reference, humans have 46 chromosomes (23 pairs). Telomeres are "caps" at the ends of chromosomes. They serve to protect them from fraying or becoming damaged. They also prevent the ends of the DNA from sticking to other strands. DNA is "sticky" because the nucleotides are designed to form long strands and ultimately chromosomes. What we don't want is the end of one chromosome attaching itself to the end of another. This would prevent the cell from replicating and expressing genes—a catastrophic result.

Telomeres are required for DNA to replicate, and careful study has shown that over time and repeated cell divisions, they become shorter. This shortening is due to decreased activity of telomerase, the enzyme that helps them maintain their length. When they get too short, it becomes very difficult for cells to divide, and the body is unable to repair itself. As we have all experienced, older dogs (not to mention people) do not heal or recover as well or as quickly as they did when they were younger. One of the reasons for this is the inability to replicate cells due to shortened telomeres.

Shortened telomeres are not only a result of aging but can also be due to a lack of the telomerase enzyme. While telomerase deficiency and aging are not synonymous, the result of the deficiency—an inability to maintain telomere length, subsequently leading to cellular dysfunction—illuminates the importance of telomeres to health and longevity. In humans, telomerase deficiency is associated with early onset of diseases such as pulmonary fibrosis (scarring of the lungs due to a failure to create normal lung tissue) and aplastic anemia (inability to make new red blood cells). In animal models, telomerase deficiency leads to cellular senescence (another of the 14 hallmarks) and accelerated aging. There is—as always—balance in the body. Maintaining long telomeres is great in that they allow cells to effectively replicate to create new tissues and keep the body healthy. In the wrong cells, however, long telomeres can lead to unregulated cellular replication, which may indicate cancer.

Given this information, one could logically assume telomere length could be used as a measure of aging. While it has been used in precisely this way for years, recent studies do cast some doubt on telomere length as a biomarker for age. In other words, maintaining long telomeres is not directly predictive of a long life span. That said, there is still significant value in measuring telomere length within the larger picture of aging and longevity. We will discuss this as a diagnostic test and its applications in Chapter 2.

Epigenetic Alterations

Every individual's genome is unique to them, with the exception of identical twins, who share a genome. (Puppies in the same litter are rarely, if ever, identical twins. They may look the same, but they are fraternal twins and do not share a common genome.) From the moment of fertilization, the genome of that individual is set in stone. Nothing in the natural world can change it other than errors in DNA replication.

If the essentially immutable genome was the whole "health and longevity" story, many individuals would be in trouble. It is quite common for dogs to carry genes that predispose them to degenerative conditions and even disease like cancer. But your dog's genome is not their destiny.

Think of the genome as an actor's script. Although there are specific words in the script, the actor may take some creative license, choosing how to emphasize certain phrases or even skipping some altogether. The same thing occurs in your dog's body. The body decides which genes to express and which to keep silent. This aggregate of expressed and unexpressed genes is referred to as the *epigenome*, or *epigenetics*. Unlike the genome, the epigenome changes over time. These changes can be due to nutrition, supplementation, exposure to toxins, the aging process, and so on. So, while we can't change your dog's genome, we can affect epigenetics, and epigenetics ultimately controls which genes are and aren't expressed in the body. One of the goals we're trying to accomplish in the quest for longevity for dogs is finding ways to maintain an epigenetic profile that looks like that of a young, healthy dog, regardless of how chronologically old they are.

Many factors influence a body's specific expression of genes, but we're going to focus on DNA methylation. It turns out that DNA isn't really just a long string of nucleotide bases. Other molecules and chemical compounds are frequently bound to DNA, and these compounds often have impacts on gene expression (that is, epigenetics). Methyl groups, which are nothing more than a carbon atom with three hydrogen atoms attached, frequently bind to specific areas on DNA. DNA methylation can be used as a marker of epigenetic age through tests called *DNA methylation clocks.*[5] Unlike your dog's chronological age, DNA methylation age can be reversed to a certain extent through specific therapies. We will discuss methylation clocks and their value to longevity science in Chapter 2. Suffice it to say that while DNA methylation age is not a reliable predictor of life span, it is a highly effective tool to quantify the efficacy of longevity-focused therapies.

Loss of Proteostasis

Quick refresher: DNA codes for genes (the genome), and there are various mechanisms that regulate which genes in the genome are expressed (the epigenome). The epigenome codes for the formation of specific proteins, which serve an incredibly wide variety of purposes encompassing just about all functions in the body, from the immune system to how food is metabolized, and so forth. This spectrum of proteins created by your dog's body is known as the *proteome.*

You can think of proteins as intricately folded origami. One piece of paper can be folded infinite ways to achieve a variety of animals and shapes, but if you want a crane, it has to be folded in one specific way. Similarly, proteins must be folded correctly to be functional. Misfolded proteins lead to disruption of the body's ability to maintain health, and in humans, their buildup is associated with aging and age-related conditions like Alzheimer's, Parkinson's, and cataracts. Not surprisingly, the body has developed ways to either refold misfolded proteins to make them functional again or break them apart and recycle their components to make new proteins. The ability of the body to maintain proper folding of proteins is known as *proteostasis*, and improving proteostasis has been shown to delay conditions associated with aging. We will discuss how to support this process in our dogs in upcoming chapters.

Deregulated Nutrient Sensing

Food, along with water and oxygen, provides the essential building blocks to grow, repair, and maintain body systems. In addition to serving as a substrate for these processes, food—its presence or absence—is responsible for a cascade of biochemical interactions.

Some studies show evidence that a reduced-calorie diet has effects on the body that can boost longevity through a variety of mechanisms, including promoting autophagy, decreasing cellular senescence, and increasing insulin sensitivity.[6] All of these things allow the body to function more like a young, healthy body rather than an aging one. Some folks have taken this information and run with it by severely restricting their own calorie intake in the hopes of living longer. The reality? Though calorie restriction plays a role, you have already seen that aging is affected by multiple biological processes, and therefore there's never going to be a "do this one thing" solution. Using calorie restriction as a standalone means of promoting longevity only results in a really, really hungry dog.

Instead, examining what happens when we restrict calories can bring the picture of longevity for dogs into clearer focus. The term *nutrient sensing* refers to the body's biochemical response to food. For example, when your dog eats, it triggers the release of compounds such as growth hormone, insulin, and insulin-like growth factor. All these compounds assist in properly assimilating the consumed nutrients so the body can grow and maintain itself. However, cellular growth and metabolism also lead to cellular damage and, subsequently, aging.

Deregulated nutrient sensing refers to the state where the body is not responding appropriately to cycles of eating and not eating, is unable to remain in balance, and ages as a result. While the balance of nutrient sensing is affected by many factors, I want to introduce three useful proteins that we will be targeting when we discuss treatment options to promote longevity in your dog.

First, *mammalian target of rapamycin* (mTOR) is a protein that encourages the crucial processes of cell growth and repair.[7] The presence of this protein increases as your dog eats and exercises. But too much mTOR is implicated in a variety of aging pathways as well as an increase in cancer risk. In short, you want mTOR to be "on" some of the time but not too much of the time.

Then, the counterbalances to mTOR are *activated protein kinases* (AMPKs), which are triggered by calorie restriction and exercise, and *sirtuins*, a group of proteins that can be activated by fasting as well as certain foods such as green tea, kale, and olive oil. Where mTOR builds things up through cellular growth and proliferation, AMPK breaks things down and helps rid the body of old, damaged, or otherwise malfunctioning cells. Sirtuins are similar, although they also play a role in repairing and stabilizing DNA damage. This is critical because all that old and damaged material promotes aging. Think of it this way: The house or apartment you live in needs periodic maintenance. Things become damaged—wood rots, roofs leak, and so on. That damaged material must be removed (AMPK) before it can be replaced with new materials (mTOR). You can't repair the house without removing the damaged material first, but neither can you live in the house with all the damaged items removed but not repaired. The key to longevity is creating and maintaining balance between building up and breaking down.

Mitochondrial Dysfunction

Mitochondria might be a term you remember from high-school biology, where it is often termed the "powerhouse of the cell." Mitochondria are the structures inside cells that, through a series of chemical processes, produce a compound called ATP that provides the necessary energy for the cell to conduct its business.

One fun fact you might not have learned in bio class: Millions of years ago mitochondria were free-living bacteria that, over time, evolved into a symbiotic relationship inside other cells. Although they are now most decidedly part of the cell, mitochondria retain their own DNA that is separate and distinct from the DNA that makes up chromosomes in the cell's nucleus. While the DNA in the nucleus of your dog's cells is a combination from Mom and Dad, mitochondrial DNA is directly inherited only from the mother. Admit it—biology is kind of cool.

You don't need a Ph.D. to recognize that if the power generators in cells aren't functioning well, there are going to be problems. Specifically, the problem is a lack of ATP, which means cellular systems can't operate at their best. Mitochondrial dysfunction can be caused by genetic factors as well as exposure to certain toxins, and the resultant lack of energy leads to cellular dysfunction and damage, potentially cancer, and—yes—aging.

Cellular Senescence

There are a lot of things that can go wrong with a cell. After all, these microscopic structures are an incredibly complex array of intracellular components, moving parts, and chemical interactions. Many of the previous hallmarks of aging cover some of the ways cells can get into trouble. As if this isn't enough, cells can become damaged due to toxins, infection, or trauma.

Cells have a variety of tools at their disposal to repair DNA, adjust epigenetics, and fix or recycle proteins to maintain proteostasis. But what happens when the cell is beyond repair? When cells get to the point of no return regarding loss of function, they can become *senescent* and are sometimes referred to as "ghost cells." Senescence means the cell is still living, but it no longer carries out many of the metabolic functions it was originally designed for. The final result of the various hallmarks of aging is often an overabundance of senescent cells.

Cellular senescence is good news and bad news (here is that balance thing again). The good news is that when the damaged cell shuts down, it is unable to reproduce and create more damaged cells that could transform into cancer. So, keeping these cells quiet can be a very good thing. All bodies, young and old, have some senescent cells, although as the body ages, it accumulates more. The number of senescent cells in a body is referred to as its "senescent cell burden." And here comes the bad news: As these cells accumulate, they can lead to problems such as decreased tissue function, inflammation, and stem cell exhaustion (another of the hallmarks). These cells may also secrete chemical compounds that promote inflammation or damage in adjacent cells. As a result, senescent cells may stimulate neighboring cells to convert to a senescent state as well, further reducing the number of functional cells in the body.

As the body ages and loses its regenerative capacity due to genomic instability, telomere attrition, cellular senescence, and so on, fewer and fewer functioning cells remain. Over time, this leads to decreased function of the body as a whole. We will discuss measuring senescent cell burden as a tool for longevity therapies in Chapter 2.

Stem Cell Exhaustion

So far, we have covered many of the ways cells make new cells and how they can repair themselves or shut down if they are irrevocably broken. Beyond these mechanisms, the body has another method for creating new cells and new tissues, one that I am sure you have heard of: *stem cells.*

Stem cells are special because they can do something no others can: transform themselves into different types of cells. What we call fully differentiated cells have a very specific function. Take a heart cell as an example. In this case, heart cells make up the tissues that allow the heart to beat. A heart cell cannot suddenly be transformed into a kidney cell; there is no mechanism in the body to do this. Stem cells, sometimes called *progenitor cells,* are considered undifferentiated because they have the ability to become other, more specialized cells, such as heart or kidney cells. Just as an unsculpted block of clay has the potential to be transformed into an endless variety of vases, sculptures, or spoon rests, so too do stem cells have the ability to become more specific and specialized, such as heart, kidney, or bone cells.

You have undoubtedly heard about stem cell therapy, where stem cells are administered to a patient to encourage the healing of an illness or injury. Stem cell therapy has been used for years in veterinary medicine to treat arthritis in dogs. The stem cells are injected into an affected joint (or injected intravenously) and will transform themselves into cartilage and other cell types that help support and repair the damage. This therapy is a big piece of a field called *regenerative medicine.*

A loss of viable stem cells is a big part of aging. The body can create new stem cells through certain supplements, some pharmaceuticals, and nutritional strategies, although generally they decline with age, as well as due to poor nutrition, toxin exposure, and other factors. On the whole, however, the older your dog gets, the fewer stem cells they have, and thus the less their body is able to build and repair tissues and maintain a healthy immune system. When a dog's body reaches the point where damage and dysfunction is outpacing its repair mechanisms and reserve of stem cells, the body begins to decline and display signs of aging.

Altered Intercellular Communication

Did you know cells in the body talk to one another? Communication between cells is actually a crucial method to maintain coordinated functioning throughout the body. The previous eight hallmarks of aging we have discussed all involve things that individual cells are doing. This ninth hallmark is about changes in communication between cells.

When we refer to *intercellular communication,* we are mostly talking about chemical signaling—such as from hormones, cytokines, and other compounds—although neuronal (electrical) communication happens as well. When cells lose the ability to communicate, they concurrently lose their ability to respond to the needs of the body.

As previously mentioned, as the body ages, the increasing population of senescent cells secrete compounds that signal neighboring cells to become senescent as well. This is sometimes referred to as *contagious aging* and is a type of altered intercellular communication. Whereas originally cellular senescence was caused by irreparable damage to a cell, thanks to secretory senescent cells, functioning cells are now being recruited too.

In upcoming chapters, we will discuss how intercellular communication can be improved through the use of nutrition, supplementation, and pharmaceuticals.

Compromised Autophagy

When your dog has not eaten for a period of time, different biochemical pathways are set in motion that promote a process called *autophagy*. Since new nutrients aren't coming in, the body has to work with what it's got, and damaged cells are consumed and recycled. Ultimately, there are biological benefits and costs to both eating and not eating. In order to maintain health and optimal function, the body needs to be able to create and build new cells and tissues. Everything in the body has a life span, however, and there are ways of cleaning up old and damaged cells in order to replace them with new and better-functioning ones. Promoting good health and longevity relies on an appropriate balance.

The process of autophagy, by which the body consumes parts of itself, may sound a little gross, but I assure you, it is absolutely necessary for all living beings. Consider it this way . . . if you have a loaf of old, moldy bread at home and you buy a new, fresh loaf, would you put the new loaf right next to the moldy one? Clearly you would not, because your new bread is going to get moldy much sooner than it would have had you disposed of the old bread first. With autophagy, your dog's body disposes of old and damaged cells by consuming them. This way, they can't have negative effects on neighboring healthy cells.

As one of the more recently described hallmarks of aging, compromised autophagy was previously categorized as part of the "deregulated nutrient sensing" hallmark. Autophagy directly affects most of the other hallmarks of aging, because the cells being consumed are dysfunctional, which can lead to instability and cellular senescence that can cause aging and disease. Remember, the goal of longevity on a cellular level is to maintain the body's cells in a healthy, optimally functioning state. When a cell is no longer able to serve its function, it should be removed to make room for new, healthy cells.

Microbiome Disturbance

The *microbiome* describes the population of bacteria living in the gastrointestinal tract, or gut, of dogs, people, and so forth. The fact that a healthy microbiome is critical to an individual's general health is something we have known for a long time. Recently, however, the microbiome has been directly linked to longevity and healthy aging through changes in the structural integrity of the GI tract, brain function, and levels of inflammation.[8]

We will discuss the microbiome in greater detail in upcoming chapters. For now, realize that the health of the microbes living in your dog's gut is directly related to how long and how well they are likely to live. We have to take care of those little guys!

Altered Mechanical Properties

Imagine a bucket of water balloons, where the bucket itself is full of water so the balloons are kind of suspended inside. This is how we used to think of cells and the environment they live in. The truth, not surprisingly, is quite a bit more complex. There are actually scaffoldlike structures both within and between the cells that create form and provide proteins and other components with the ability to move around. These structures make up kind of a highway system, allowing the transport of compounds from one area of a cell to another or from one cell to another. In addition, some cells, such as white blood cells, need to move around in order to keep the body healthy. Just like when a bridge is out and you have to drive an hour out of your way to get home, when this cellular infrastructure becomes disrupted, the body is not able to operate optimally, which in turn leads to dysfunction and aging. The study of these mechanical functions is known as "mechanobiology," and while it is relatively new, it shows a lot of promise in the field of longevity science.

Splicing Dysregulation

We have previously discussed how errors in DNA (genomic instability) and altered structure of DNA (epigenetic alterations) contribute to aging. We also discussed loss of proteostasis, meaning proteins are "misfolded," leading to nonfunctional or abnormally functioning proteins. Another closely related factor is dysregulation of RNA. While DNA holds the "master genetic code," RNA is the "middleman" who reads the DNA and ultimately creates the proteins that the DNA codes for. When changes arise in RNA, splicing dysregulation occurs, and the integrity of the proteins that are formed is compromised, which can lead to protein dysfunction, disease, and aging.

Inflammation

One of the most prominent features of aging is the increase in inflammation throughout the body. This process, sometimes called *inflammaging,* is caused by tissue damage, immune system dysfunction, an inability to "clean up" damaged or senescent cells, pro-inflammatory secretions from senescent cells, and other factors. In short, there are a lot of causes of chronic inflammation, but what they have in common is furthering cellular damage and preventing cells from being able to appropriately communicate. While inflammation has long been known to be a contributor to aging, it was previously categorized within "altered intercellular communication." Given how prominent a role inflammation plays in the aging process, the scientific community has decided it warrants being considered a hallmark of aging in its own right.

UNDERSTANDING THE ROOT CAUSE

When I was in veterinary school, my professors were quick to correct students who implied that a patient's condition was due to their age. "Age is not a disease," they would say. *Merriam-Webster* defines *disease* as "a condition of the living animal or plant body or of one of its parts that impairs normal functioning and is typically manifested by distinguishing signs and symptoms."[9] Based on this definition and what you now understand about the 14 hallmarks of aging, what do you think? Is aging a disease?

If it isn't, then we accept it as an inevitability and do little or nothing to stop it. Conversely, if it is a disease, we can approach treating and curing it like we do any other medical condition. First, we find out what causes it—the

14 hallmarks are an excellent foundation for this. Once we understand the underlying causes, we can set about the task of finding ways to prevent, treat, or at least limit the progression of this disease that affects every living thing on the planet. This is the basis of modern longevity science. So, how do we combat aging? More specifically, how do we approach maintaining health and youthful vigor for far longer than is currently considered normal?

One of the most critical steps in the quest for longevity is a step that, unfortunately, isn't taken often enough in the field of medicine. Each patient needs to be evaluated and treated as an individual. Yes, there are some through lines with medicine and longevity science. For example, it is important to keep inflammation in check in all dogs. That said, each individual has their own strengths and weaknesses based on both internal factors (like the epigenome) and external factors (like exposure to environmental toxins). One dog may be prone to kidney disease based on their genetics or environmental factors, whereas another may be more at risk for arthritis.

Allopathic medicine tends to take a two-dimensional view when it comes to treatment. Physicians and veterinarians are taught to treat a diagnosis. They rarely discuss the underpinnings of the diagnosis. What genetic, environmental, or other variables led to the dog developing the condition? Although it may sound completely obvious, this is just not how doctors are trained. Allopathic medicine in general is geared toward treating the symptoms of disease without gaining an understanding of how to address the root cause. Granted, some of this is a function of doctors being overworked and not having the time to do a deep dive into each individual patient. In a more fundamental sense, however, allopathic medicine has evolved into a paradigm that doesn't spend a lot of time on prevention.

While there are pharmaceutical interventions we will discuss within the context of longevity medicine, a lot of what we will talk about are preventive measures that don't generate a lot of revenue for either doctors or the pharmaceutical industry. And, if we are having an honest discussion here, the direction the medical profession takes is heavily influenced by the money behind Big Pharma.

To combat aging, we have to look at methods of testing, or quantifying, the processes that cause it, as well as metrics by which we can measure how a dog is aging in terms of their unique body. We can use these diagnostic tests to determine what specific areas each individual dog may need help with. The treatments may look like diet or nutritional changes, supplements, pharmaceuticals, and even interventional medical procedures. It all depends on what the individual needs.

A friend and colleague, Jeffrey Gladden, M.D., is one of the world's leading physicians in performance and antiaging medicine (for humans). He does extensive testing for his patients and then designs customized treatment protocols to improve their health and longevity. Because of the cutting-edge and constantly evolving nature of the science of aging, he is fond of saying, "We shouldn't be married to the answers; we should be married to the questions." This is a profound statement. Doctors are trained to seek answers, but the truth—as so often is the case in life—is only found after you ask the right questions.

Not asking the right questions is sometimes a function of a doctor pursuing an incorrect diagnostic or treatment pathway. For example, I recently had a canine patient, Roy, come into my office who had seen multiple veterinarians for chronic skin problems, including itching and recurring infections. He had been "worked up" for allergies and treated with medication, but the problem always returned. It was only when I tested him and found out he had low thyroid function that we were able to permanently resolve his skin problems.

When it comes to longevity, however, not asking the right questions is more frequently an issue of doctors not knowing what questions to ask. When my professor said, "Age is not a disease," what he was really saying was "Don't ask about the specific pathways that cause aging and how we can intervene." It's not that my professor was closed-minded . . . that is how he was taught and how all doctors are taught. The current paradigm of Western medicine is that aging is an inevitability. We can try to treat the cancer, the heart disease, the kidney failure, and so on but not the underpinnings of why the body breaks down as we (and our pets) age. The questions that longevity science is asking are the questions that are going to allow us to "turn the corner" and prevent, or reverse, aging. Instead of treating the symptoms of aging (cancer, organ disease, and so forth), we will learn to prevent and treat the processes that lead to the diseases (symptoms) that ultimately end with bodily decline and death. These are the "answers" we seek. We, meaning modern medicine, must reframe our questions to get to the root cause of aging and not merely treat symptoms.

* * *

You now have a foundational understanding of many of the factors that cause the body to age and deteriorate. In truth, there are more than 14, and we will touch on a few others throughout our journey. From a treatment perspective, there are also many approaches to promote longevity because, as you have seen, aging is not caused by one single issue. We have to address as many of the hallmarks of aging as we can if we hope to achieve success, and the key is in maintaining balance in the body.

We will explore how to leverage nutrition, exercise, integrative medicine, specific supplements, therapies, and regenerative medicine. Equally important is a discussion of what you should avoid. And because the field of longevity science is expanding and making new discoveries all the time, we will discuss research and breakthroughs that point to what will become available in the near future to allow your dog to live an even longer and healthier life! In the next chapter we'll take a look at some of the diagnostic tests that can not only determine any potential problems in your dog but also help you measure how well certain interventions are working.

The Hallmarks of Aging*

* Reprinted from *Cell,* Volume 153/Issue 6, Carlos López-Otín, Maria A. Blasco, Linda Partridge, Manuel Serrano, and Guido Kroemer, "The Hallmarks of Aging," pages 1194–1217, copyright 2013, with permission from Elsevier.

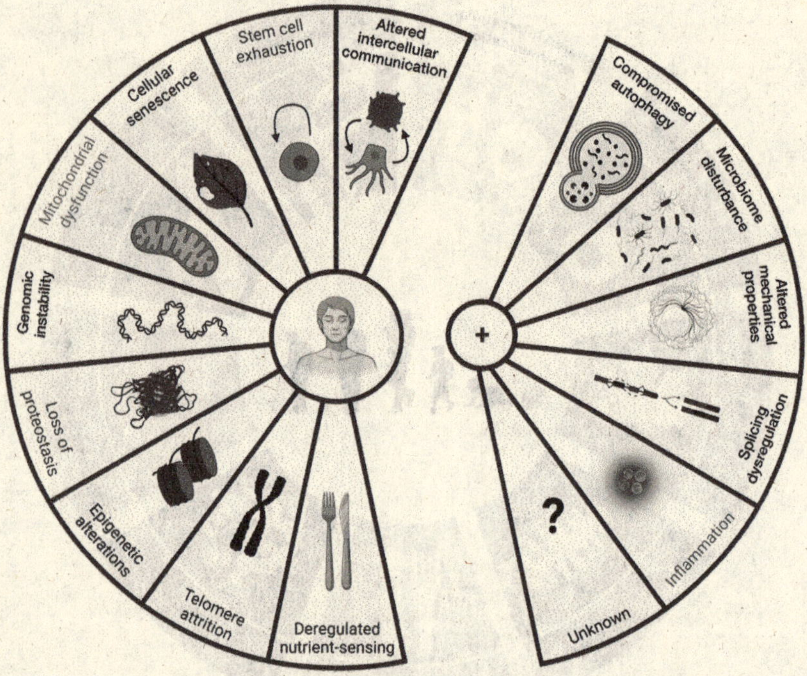

New Hallmarks of Ageing*

* © 2022 Schmauck-Medina et al. (CC by 3.0) Schmauck-Medina T, Molière A, Lautrup S, Zhang J, Chlopicki S, Madsen HB, Cao S, Soendenbroe C, Mansell E, Vestergaard MB, Li Z, Shiloh Y, Opresko PL, Egly JM, Kirkwood T, Verdin E, Bohr VA, Cox LS, Stevnsner T, Rasmussen LJ, Fang EF. "New hallmarks of ageing: a 2022 Copenhagen ageing meeting summary." *Aging* (Albany NY). 2022 Aug 29;14(16):6829– 6839. doi: 10.18632/aging.204248. Epub 2022 Aug 29. PMID: 36040386; PMCID: PMC9467401.

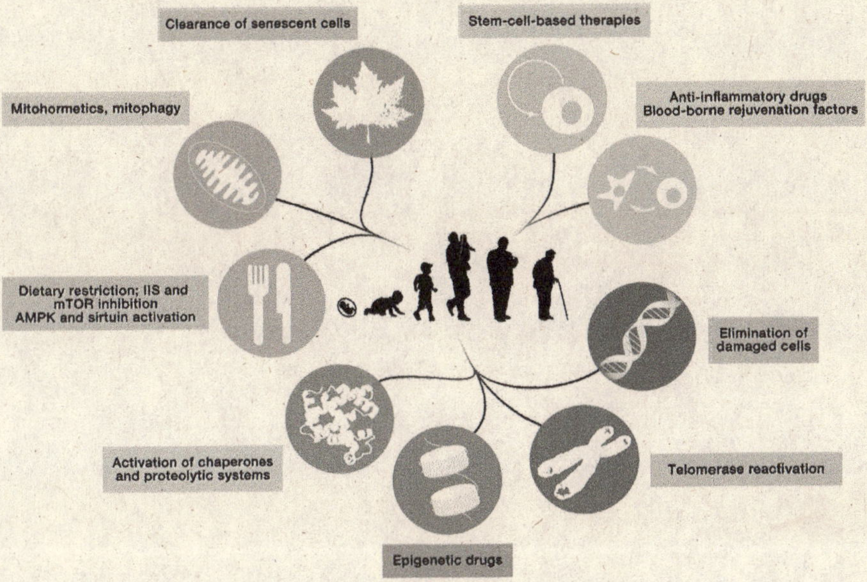

Interventions That Might Extend Human Healthspan*

* Reprinted from *Cell,* Volume 153/Issue 6, Carlos López-Otín, Maria A. Blasco, Linda Partridge, Manuel Serrano, and Guido Kroemer, "The Hallmarks of Aging," pages 1194–1217, copyright 2013, with permission from Elsevier.

CHAPTER 2

DIAGNOSTIC TESTING

Ponce de León and all those who came before and after him failed in the quest for immortality because they weren't asking the right questions. They didn't have the understanding we now do of what aging really is. It turns out that "Could someone please direct me to the magic fountain of immortality?" is not going to solve the longevity puzzle. That said, given what he had to work with at the time, it was about as good a question as any.

Only recently has the scientific community begun to uncover the means with which to ask the right questions and thus uncover the right answers. After all, the human genome was fully mapped only in 2003, and almost everything we are discussing in this book has been discovered in the last 20 years.[1] With the foundation of the 14 hallmarks that contribute to aging, the next logical question is: What can we do with this knowledge? In other words, how do we leverage the information to help our dogs live longer, healthier lives?

As we have discussed, aging is not caused by one single issue. It happens because of a compilation of many processes in the body that, over time, lead to diminished ability to heal and regenerate tissues, decreased immune system function, and increased incidence of cancer. While the susceptibility to disease, such as cancer, and other degenerative processes is a challenge all dogs face, the specifics of their health strengths and weaknesses vary from one dog to the next due to their individual genome. This is where diagnostic testing becomes part of the longevity story.

The newness of understanding how the genome, epigenome, proteome, and so on affect aging is the reason why the discussion of longevity is so fascinating right now. For the first time in human history, we are uncovering the processes that cause aging and finding ways to measure them. And if you can measure them, then you can look for treatments that make the measurements better and, subsequently, keep your dog youthful and healthy. Remember, testing is not only about finding out what your dog is susceptible to but also about monitoring their progress once aging interventions (diet, supplements, medications, and treatments) have begun, so we know what is working and how to make our dogs physiologically younger. In this chapter we'll take a look at some current diagnostic-testing options, such as blood-count and chemistry panels; genetic testing; and screening for specific medical conditions, food sensitivities, and overall gut health so that you can make the best health decisions for your individual dog. I'll also explain some of the exciting new tests for humans and some dogs, like measuring oxidative stress or detecting cancer, so that you can be prepared to utilize them now or when they become available for dogs in the future.

TESTING OPTIONS FOR TODAY

Until recently, there were few, if any, diagnostic tests that would allow us to even begin to ask the critical questions surrounding aging. If I had written this book 10—or even 5—years ago, the number of available options for diagnostic testing would be a fraction of what they are now. And 10 years from now? Oh boy—wait until you see what is coming!

Because of the rapidly changing landscape of available diagnostic testing related to aging, I've divided this chapter between discussing what testing is available for your dog right now and what is coming in the near future: the next 5 or 10 years. Given the rapidity with which the science is progressing, it may be even sooner than that.

The vast majority of diagnostic testing in veterinary medicine in the United States is done through two labs, IDEXX and Antech. Most of the more longevity-focused testing is performed by other, smaller laboratories that are not necessarily what the veterinary profession might describe as mainstream. To be clear, these smaller labs are highly qualified and provide reliable and actionable results for those who understand how to interpret them. Not being "mainstream" in this context means that most veterinarians are probably not aware of them, because they utilize only IDEXX or Antech for lab services. As we move through the tests, I'll provide you with the names of the laboratories offering them so you can discuss them with your veterinarian. Hopefully, if they are open-minded, they will be willing to explore some new avenues of diagnosis and ultimately treatment. I also provide a brief explanation of what the test is for as well as how it fits into the longevity puzzle. Wherever possible, I'll let you know which of the hallmarks of aging apply to that specific test.

Standard Blood Panels

The place to begin our discussion of the diagnostic options currently available to your dog is with the routine blood panels your veterinarian runs every day. The cornerstone of laboratory screening in veterinary (and human) medicine is the complete blood count (CBC) and chemistry panel. These tests are the primary means by which modern medicine evaluates the health of a patient, and many medical conditions can be diagnosed and monitored through this type of screening. It is important to understand what these tests can and cannot tell us about your dog's health, as there are lots of misconceptions among pet owners about what can be determined from a standard blood panel.

Blood is composed of cells suspended in liquid. The cells—red blood cells, white blood cells, and platelets—are evaluated by the CBC. Changes in number can indicate significant medical problems like anemia, infection, inflammation, and autoimmune disease, among others. Serum, on the other hand, is the liquid component of the blood and is evaluated in a chemistry panel. Chem panels are able to look at parameters of organ function such as those of the liver and kidneys as well as hydration, electrolytes, blood proteins, fats, and so on. Changes in these values can indicate poor organ function, endocrine (hormonal) imbalances, dehydration, and other disease processes. Beyond standard blood chemistries, your veterinarian has access to hundreds of other tests used to diagnose specific issues, such as abnormalities in thyroid function, screening for pancreatitis, indicators of heart disease, and so forth. The CBC and chemistry panel and the various other available ancillary tests are highly valuable diagnostic tools for your veterinarian to look at the overall health of your dog, and they should continue to be so.

As with every diagnostic test, there are limitations. While a "normal-looking" CBC and chemistry panel is a good indicator of health, it is not a measure of how old your dog is or how fast they are aging. In fact, veterinarians routinely see geriatric dogs whose blood work looks fantastic, yet the dog is infirmed with age-related disease and may not have much time left. Perhaps the most glaring shortfall of a CBC and chemistry panel is its inability to diagnose nearly all cancers. Many people assume if their dog has cancer, it will show up in a routine blood test. But it almost never does. Unless we are talking about a cancer of the blood such as leukemia, most dogs with cancer will have normal blood panels (but see more on cancer testing later in this chapter).

Getting back to the concept of asking the right questions, diagnostic testing is our means of asking the questions that will lead us to the answers to better health and longevity. A CBC, a chem panel, and the other tests often included in a routine workup ask specific questions that frequently provide valuable answers. While the information *is* valuable, we should not make the mistake of assuming there aren't a lot more questions to ask.

Genetic Testing

Recall that the sequence of DNA unique to every individual is called the genome. The genes in the DNA code for proteins that affect how the body functions. But not every gene in the DNA is transcribed into proteins. The spectrum of genes that are expressed is known as the epigenome. While treatments such as gene therapy will someday be able to change the genome of an organism, for our purposes, think of the genome as something largely written in stone. Your dog was born with their genome, and, barring errors in DNA replication, it will be the same throughout their life.

It is now possible to evaluate our dogs for specific genetic markers that let us know what genes they have in their DNA. This is beneficial because some genes confer benefits to health and longevity, while others may predispose your dog to specific medical conditions. Understanding your dog's specific genetic markers can help us keep an eye out for specific problems they may be prone to. While the genome is written in stone, the epigenome is not. In other words, even though your dog may have a gene that has the potential to lead to problems, there may be things we can do to limit, or even prevent, its expression. Within the context of the hallmarks of aging, this fits into epigenetic alterations. If a deleterious gene is not being expressed, it can do no harm.

The two most common commercial genetic-marker tests in dogs are from Wisdom Panel and Embark. Both companies offer a screening that can tell you what breed(s) your dog is and evaluate over 200 potential markers for disease. In addition, many veterinary schools have genetics laboratories that run specific testing. For example, the veterinary school at the University of California–Davis runs genetics panels for specific breeds, as many purebreds are associated with a predisposition to certain conditions.

As previously noted, just because a dog carries a gene for a disease does not mean they do, or ever will, have the disease. Since your dog's DNA is a combination of contributions from Mom and Dad, they have two copies of each gene, and the risk of disease has to do with the genes being the same (homozygous) or different (heterozygous) and if they are dominant or recessive.

In cases where symptoms suggest a specific medical condition but there is no definitive diagnosis, knowing if a dog carries a certain gene can be very helpful. For example, there is a condition in dogs called degenerative myelopathy (DM). DM is similar to ALS (Lou Gehrig's disease) in people. There is no way to definitively diagnose DM, but we can run a test for genetic markers in dogs that are showing some symptoms and find out if they are a carrier. If they carry one or more copies of the DM gene, it is possible they have DM. If they don't have the gene, it is not possible for them to have the disease, and DM can be ruled out.

In addition to confirming or ruling out a diagnosis, testing genetic markers allows us to know what the dog may be prone to in the future so we are aware of what to look out for. Also, for any breeders, it is critical to know what is in the parents' genetic makeup so they don't inadvertently breed dogs likely to produce offspring with genetic diseases.

Biochemical Markers of Disease

Another lab that is running some exciting diagnostics for dogs is VDI Laboratory. VDI has put together combinations of tests, many of which are not otherwise readily available, to screen for particular medical conditions in dogs and cats. Test panels include evaluation of vitamin levels and markers for inflammation, arthritis, and cancer. There are too many specific tests to discuss each one, although a few are worth highlighting, including vitamin D, magnesium, and thymidine kinase 1 (TK1).

Chances are you are vitamin D deficient—most of us are. Unfortunately, the same is true for our dogs. But unlike humans, dogs do not synthesize vitamin D from sunlight. Their vitamin D comes from dietary sources only, and even though you may be feeding an ideal diet (more on that in Chapter 3), they're probably still deficient. Easily 90 percent of the dogs I have tested in my office who are not on a vitamin D supplement are deficient.

Vitamin D is incredibly important when it comes to combating aging. It promotes autophagy, or recycling of old or damaged cells. It also inhibits mitochondrial dysfunction; decreases oxidative stress and inflammation; and inhibits epigenetic alterations, genomic instability, and telomere shortening.[2] That's at least 5 of the 14 hallmarks of aging being affected by something as commonplace as vitamin D! Correcting vitamin D deficiency is as easy as sending a little blood to the lab for testing and then supplementing as indicated based on the dog's levels. Follow-up testing to monitor levels over time is always a good idea.

Another low-hanging fruit when it comes to longevity testing is magnesium levels. Magnesium plays a role in energy metabolism, cell proliferation, apoptosis (programmed cell death), oxidative stress, and inflammation.[3] Again, just like vitamin D, this mineral affects quite a few of the hallmarks of aging, and it is easy to supplement.

TK1 is an enzyme in cells that is involved with cell division. One of the characteristics of cancer is uncontrolled or unregulated cell division leading to tumor formation, so TK1 levels can become elevated when cancer is present.[4] Not surprisingly, the earlier cancer is diagnosed in dogs, the more likely it is that treatment will be effective. Evaluating TK1 in dogs can provide insight that allows for early intervention and a greater chance at a long, healthy life.

VDI runs a variety of panels geared toward patients who have particular medical issues. An appropriate panel, such as a GI panel, arthritis panel, or cancer panel, can be enormously valuable in addition to the CBC and chem panel your veterinarian will order as a routine health screen. Remember, the value here is not only in diagnosing a disease or a vitamin or mineral deficiency but also in being able to monitor your dog's progress after treatment has begun. All dogs are individuals and respond to treatment differently. Understanding how *your* dog is responding will allow your veterinarian to tailor treatment to fit their needs.

Omega Fatty Acids

In addition to vitamin D and magnesium, omega-3 fatty acids are another critical nutrient for all pets. These beneficial fats decrease inflammation, promote circulation, support neurologic function, and aid in digestion, along with conferring a host of other benefits. Omega fatty acids are found in marine lipids such as fish oil, krill oil, and algae oil. While omega fatty acids are also found in plant sources such as flaxseed oil, they are not particularly bioavailable compared to marine sources and, as such, supplements from these sources are not recommended for your dog. A recent study evaluating the effects of omega-3 fatty acids in humans found that a one percent increase in omega-3s in the blood correlated to an almost five-year increase in life span.[5] That's a similar life-span increase to a person quitting smoking.

As is the case with vitamin D, almost every dog I test for omega-3 levels comes back deficient. Correcting the deficiency is as easy as adding some fish oil to your dog's bowl. Retesting a few months after beginning supplementation is a good idea to make sure you are giving the right amount. Omega-3 levels can be easily tested with a small blood sample through OmegaQuant.

Oxidative Stress

Undoubtedly, you have heard of antioxidants. They are popular in the supplement market for good reason.

Antioxidants can help protect tissues from damage caused by oxidation. The body produces its own antioxidants, and in a perfect world, there is a balance (there's that word again) between oxidation and antioxidants. So, to be clear, oxidation is a vital process that helps rid the body of damaged or even cancerous cells. Problems, however, do occur when the level of oxidation is out of balance with the body's ability to counteract it. Excessive oxidation in the body is called *oxidative stress* and is, among other things, a cause of the aging hallmark mitochondrial dysfunction.[6]

Hemopet has developed a test, CellBIO, that measures levels of a compound called isoprostane in the saliva of your dog.[7] To make a long story short, isoprostane is produced when essential fatty acids (like omega-3s) undergo oxidative damage. Thus, isoprostane, and subsequently the CellBIO test, can be used as a measurement of oxidative stress and how it can improve over time when treated.

Inflammation from Food

As I've touched upon, inflammation can have negative effects on intercellular communication, which contributes to aging. Hemopet has another saliva-based test called NutriScan that measures antibodies, specifically IgA and IgM, and how they react to certain food ingredients.[8] This test gives you an idea of which foods your dog has a sensitivity to and will lead to inflammation in the gut. There are other food-sensitivity tests out there, some using saliva and others using blood. None of these tests are 100 percent accurate when it comes to determining the foods your dog is sensitive to, but in my experience, NutriScan is the most reliable food-sensitivity test available.

Clearly, the benefit of diagnostic testing is that it helps eliminate guesswork. I'm sorry to say that sometimes treatment decisions in medicine are "educated guesses," based on how other patients have historically responded to treatment. This is true regardless of whether we are talking about allergies, GI problems, cancer, or any number of other conditions. It is also true for both allopathic medicine and holistic care. When we can test for something specific, however, it allows us to take more direct and effective action.

In my office, it is an everyday occurrence for a pet owner to bring in an animal with a chronic condition where conventional medical treatment has failed. There are many reasons for this, but the most common is that the pet is diagnosed with a condition that has a lot of possible underlying causes. For example, I recently saw a dog in my office named Ocean. Ocean had chronic allergies that led to biting and scratching, which was keeping his owners awake at night. Ocean routinely developed focal skin infections, *hot spots*, that required treatment as well. The veterinarians who had previously treated Ocean used medications and prescription diets to help, but these efforts met with only partial success, and every time the treatment was stopped, his allergies grew worse again.

Generally, people and animals have allergic reactions to something in their environment (dust, pollen, and the like), something they are eating, or both. While statistically environmental allergies are most common, food frequently plays a part. Given the extensive efforts that had already been made with Ocean, I decided it would be a good idea to run a food-sensitivity test to see if this could be part of his problem. When the test came back, it was clear Ocean had sensitivities to wheat, rice, beef, salmon, and chicken. When I looked through his medical history, I found that even when Ocean's diet had been changed in the past, he was always eating at least one of those ingredients. I converted him to a fresh, whole-food diet using pork as a protein, and within weeks he was feeling better, and he stopped developing the hot spots. He still had a tendency to get itchy, but the severity was improved by at least 80 percent. It was the diagnostic testing that allowed us to finally find the key to getting Ocean better.

Microbiome

You may have heard about the relationship of gut health to overall health, and now you know disturbances in the microbiome are considered a hallmark of aging. This has a lot to do with the fact that 70 to 80 percent of the immune cells in your dog's (and your own) body are in the gastrointestinal tract.[9] An unhealthy microbiome leads to inflammation, poor nutrient absorption, and decreased mitochondrial function, which affect the function of the entire body. There is also a definitive link between gut health and brain health, known as the *gut–brain axis*. Thus, it will probably come as no surprise to you that the makeup of the bacterial population in the gut, known as the microbiome, plays a part in your dog's longevity. In humans, we already know that specific microbiome patterns are correlated with longevity.[10]

When it comes to our dogs, there are two diagnostic labs available to evaluate their microbiome. Texas A&M University's veterinary school runs a test called a *dysbiosis index*, and AnimalBiome will run your dog's full microbiome. The A&M dysbiosis index measures specific bacteria in a stool sample and provides information regarding the health of your dog's microbiome. This test can be particularly valuable for dogs with chronic gastrointestinal disease or, really, any kind of chronic illness. AnimalBiome's testing also looks at the spectrum of microflora (bacteria) in your dog's GI tract. In both cases, abnormalities in the microbiome can be a cause and a symptom of a host of issues affecting quality and quantity of life. So much of the immune system is in the gut that seemingly unrelated diseases, like allergies, autoimmune conditions, cognitive impairment, and others, may trace at least some of their origins to the microbiome. We will discuss ways to improve your dog's microbiome in Chapters 3 and 6.

Cancer

I mentioned earlier that one of the large drawbacks to blood tests is the inability to detect cancer. Since one in four dogs will get cancer in their lifetime, this is a serious problem.[11] Given that a similar problem exists in human medicine, a lot of resources have been put forth to find a solution.

The liquid biopsy is the next big thing in cancer diagnostics. Generally, a biopsy is the removal of a piece of tissue for the purposes of analyzing it, usually to determine if it is cancerous. The problem with biopsies is they can be difficult, costly, and taxing on the body, as they require anesthesia, surgery, and recovery time. The other problem is that, in its earliest stages, cancer has no symptoms, meaning you don't have any indication a biopsy is necessary, much less what tissue you are supposed to collect, until the cancer is more advanced and potentially more dangerous. Liquid biopsy aims to fix this problem.

Technically not a real biopsy, the liquid biopsy is a blood sample that is analyzed for circulating tumor DNA (ctDNA). You see, when cancer is present, cancerous cells or pieces of cells break off and travel through the bloodstream. When whole cancer cells enter the blood, the cancer metastasizes (spreads). This test offers the opportunity to find cancer earlier than we otherwise would, as well as to monitor if a cancer patient is in remission.

While liquid biopsies are receiving a lot of focus and research dollars in human medicine, PetDx is the first company in the veterinary field to offer the test for dogs. This is very exciting, because early diagnosis of cancer is the key to successful treatment. As with everything in life, however, the devil is in the details, and there are some shortcomings with the current technology.

In scientific terms, the accuracy of a test is measured by its sensitivity and specificity. *Sensitivity* refers to the likelihood a test will read positive when the sample is actually positive (in this case, detection of cancer). *Specificity* refers to the likelihood a test will read negative when the sample is negative. In other words, is it coming up with false positives in dogs that don't actually have cancer? The good news about the PetDx test is that in a published study, the specificity was found to be 98.5 percent—there are very few false-positive results, and a negative result is very likely to mean the dog does not have cancer. The not-so-good news is the sensitivity was 54.7 percent, meaning that cancer was actually detected in only a little more than half of the positive samples.[12]

In this case, the correctly diagnosed samples were almost exclusively from dogs with known cancer. (To be fair, the study also found cancer in four dogs who had not previously been diagnosed.) This matters because if the cancer is already diagnosable through more conventional means, the blood test isn't really all that valuable. The ideal is diagnosing at the earliest stages of cancer, before there is any detectable disease. Unfortunately, it doesn't look like the PetDx test is able to do that reliably just yet.

Despite its current shortcomings, liquid biopsy is a very promising diagnostic test that likely will become a staple in both human and veterinary medicine once the sensitivity of the test improves significantly. Billions of dollars are currently being invested into multiple companies to make this technology a reality. This is one of those problems that will be solved with money and time. Watch this space!

Testing Options for Tomorrow

There are likely more diagnostic tests focused on prolonging life span and health span than you might have thought. And, if I'm being honest, there are more available options than a general-practice veterinarian is likely to be currently utilizing. As fascinating and useful as this catalog of tests is, what is coming in the near future is even more exciting. Most of the diagnostics described in the upcoming section are already available for humans, which generally means they will become available for dogs before too long. Even though research and testing for dogs are in early stages for many of these, we can still use what we know about the affected body systems to consider and apply therapies that can increase longevity.

One note about the medical "establishment," be it human or veterinary, is that it is extremely slow to adopt new approaches to health care, especially when they run counter to long-held beliefs. The idea that aging and death are inevitable is about as deeply rooted a belief as there is in medical practice, and there will be a large segment of the medical community that will dismiss any concept suggesting otherwise as being outrageous and a fool's errand. Like everything else in medicine, however, what seems outlandish today will be accepted as mainstream tomorrow. For those of us who can see what is coming, there is no need to wait for the establishment to give us permission to help our dogs live longer than ever.

Omics

A good way to look at forthcoming diagnostic options is to sequence or order them in the same way cellular function either contributes to healthy living or aging, depending on whether or not these systems are in proper working order. Ultimately, this sequencing is a measurable series of processes called *omics* that indicates how well a body is functioning and how its functions relate to either promoting or inhibiting the aging process. We will eventually be able to measure the state of health of each one of these steps to determine where a dog's body is starting to age due to the degradation of one or more processes. The progression of the five "omes" is: genome → epigenome → transcriptome → proteome → metabolome.

- As we discussed in Chapter 1, it all starts with your dog's DNA, also referred to as their **genome**.
- Not all the genes in the DNA are expressed and transcribed into proteins. The spectrum of genes that are expressed at any given time is referred to as the **epigenome**. The expression of the genes is often referred to as epigenetics.
- In order for the epigenome to be expressed, DNA is transcribed into RNA, which is in turn translated into proteins. The full spectrum of what the cell is transcribing is called the **transcriptome**.
- The specific proteins created by the cell based on the transcriptome is called the **proteome**.
- All the proteins created by cells ultimately govern how the cells, and the whole body, function.

> The functioning of all the cells is referred to as their metabolism. Metabolic processes in the cell result in the formation of small molecules that can be measured, which gives us an idea of cellular activity and physiologic status. The aggregate of these small molecules is known as the **metabolome**.

Advanced Genome Testing

Earlier in this chapter, we discussed tests that look at portions of your dog's genome. Several private labs and universities are able to evaluate the genome and check for specific genetic markers that could indicate predisposition to specific diseases. These tests, however, examine only a tiny fraction of the entire genome.

The canine genome contains approximately 19,000 genes (the human genome contains 20,000 to 25,000). Interestingly, 14,200 of the canine genes are orthologs, meaning they share a common genetic ancestor with both humans and mice.[13, 14] This is, of course, consistent with what we know about evolution. The genetic-marker tests we reviewed earlier look at a little more than 200 genes—so, as you can see, only a tiny fraction of your dog's genes are currently being analyzed.

The truth is, no one knows what all those genes do, whether they are in your dog, yourself, a mouse, or a fruit fly. For a long time, researchers thought a lot of DNA was "junk DNA," meaning it didn't code for anything. Now it appears that scientists just didn't have a full understanding of all the functions DNA was responsible for. As time goes on, we will learn more about your dog's 19,000 genes, and you will eventually be able to run your dog's entire genome, just like you can your own. With this information, your dog's genetic tendencies will be greatly illuminated, and we will likely have the opportunity to strategically promote expression of beneficial genes and silence the ones that play a role in aging and disease—changing your dog's epigenetics. A little further down the road, gene therapy will become available to repair or replace genes that are disadvantageous to your dog's health.

The ability to change your dog's epigenetics is not far around the bend. As our dogs age, their gene expression changes, and that is a big part of aging. Remember, the epigenome is where it all starts as far as protein expression goes, and the process continues all the way down the cascade to the metabolome. Once we are able to fully evaluate the epigenome and then adjust it to reflect a younger dog, your pooch is going to be looking and acting their best for a very long time.

Epigenetic Age

One feature of the epigenome that is very, very close to being brought to light is determining dogs' epigenetic age. In Chapter 1, we briefly discussed DNA methylation clocks, which estimate age based on a blood sample. The real benefit here is, unlike chronological age, methylation age is reversible. That's right: certain therapies can actually make you or your dog appear younger based on their methylation patterns. In human medicine, DNA methylation clocks are being used to monitor responses to longevity therapies. The goal is to lower the patient's methylation age, and this is readily achievable with many different longevity interventions, ranging from diet and exercise to stem cell therapy. For all its usefulness, DNA methylation age is not directly correlated to life span. A similar test is being developed that is designed to be a specific predictor of life span. To say it another way, the test would tell you when you (or your dog) are likely to die based on your current health status. Depending on how you look at it, that could be a super useful tool or super scary. Appropriately, the name of this test is Grim Age.

DNA methylation clocks exist for both dogs and humans, although the canine version is not quite commercially available yet. Interestingly, the UCLA researcher who invented methylation clocks, Dr. Steve Horvath, has told me his dog clock is actually more accurate than the one he developed for humans. The technology is here—it's just waiting for someone to commercialize it.

Transcriptome, Proteome, and Metabolome Analysis

Evaluating the transcriptome provides insight into what genes are expressed during different medical conditions and at different stages of your dog's life. This information will offer insight into medical conditions your dog may be susceptible to and, as such, may hint at therapeutic options for treatments that may eventually become available. Transcriptome analysis is currently available for human patients, so it is on its way to the veterinary world.

Evaluating the proteome and metabolome is a little further down the road than some of the other omics. Being able to evaluate these two "omes" in an organism (human, dog, or otherwise) will provide a clearer picture of (1) exactly what proteins are being produced and (2) metabolic function and health, respectively. These evaluations are largely in the research phase at this point, and it will likely be some time before they are commercially available for dogs.

Is it really necessary to measure and monitor all five of the "omes" in the quest to promote longevity? We don't really know right now, but probably not. My prediction is that two or possibly three of them will prove to be useful predictive measures of both aging and efficacy of age-related therapies, but research is ongoing.

Telomeres

As the segments of DNA at the ends of the chromosomes, telomeres are vital to a cell's ability to replicate DNA and therefore create new cells. The older your dog gets, the shorter their telomeres become and the less able they are to repair and replace cells and tissues. Thus, aging accelerates. For a long time, as I mentioned before, it was presumed telomere length was a good prognostic indicator of longevity. It makes sense, right? Young people and animals have long telomeres and older ones have shorter telomeres, so the shorter the telomeres are, the more advanced the patient's age.

Well, science often has a few tricks up its sleeve, and current research would indicate measuring telomere length is not a great predictor of longevity.[15] The current feeling is that epigenetic age (measured by DNA methylation clocks) is more predictive, although it should be said that none of these diagnostics are rock-solid. There are trends but not absolutes, and there's no test available that will tell you how long you, or your dog, are going to live. All that said, given it is a measure of one of the hallmarks of aging, telomere length is still a useful parameter in the overall evaluation of health and longevity.

Telomere length is now commonly measured in humans who are proactive with longevity therapy. Telomeres control DNA replication, so understanding your telomere length can be a window into how able your body is to make new cells and repair itself. There are products on the market that are designed to help lengthen telomeres, so being able to measure them helps determine the efficacy of these products. A few companies are beginning to offer telomere-lengthening products and telomere testing for dogs, although it hasn't hit its stride just yet. Though the diagnostics might not be available quite yet, you can still consider therapies to help keep your dog's telomeres looking young and healthy, which we'll discuss in Chapter 6.

Plasmalogens

Though the hallmarks we've discussed provide a great outline for discussion and research, there are factors beyond them that contribute to the aging process. More and more are being discovered, and this is why the quest for longevity is finally making actual progress after thousands of years. One factor that has come to light is *plasmalogens*.

Plasmalogens are components of all cellular membranes and are in particularly high concentration in the brain, heart, lungs, kidneys, and eyes. They appear to have several functions, including serving as a source of antioxidants (limiting oxidative stress) and omega fatty acids. Plasmalogens make up about 20 percent of the cell membrane, and their presence (or absence) has a substantial impact on cellular function.[16, 17]

Research indicates plasmalogen levels decline with age and are associated with diseases such as cardiac conditions, diabetes, cancer, dementia, Parkinson's, Alzheimer's, and multiple sclerosis in humans.[18] The bottom line is that decreasing levels of plasmalogens are correlated with a higher probability of dying. There is also some evidence to suggest decreasing levels are due to mitochondrial dysfunction, which brings us back to one of the original nine hallmarks.[19, 20] Very little research into plasmalogens has been conducted in dogs as of yet, although there is every reason to believe these compounds play just as critical a role in health and aging in dogs as they do in that of us humans. Plasmalogen testing is currently available in human medicine, and there are supplements to support plasmalogen levels in the body. We will discuss ways you can support your dog's plasmalogen levels in Chapter 6.

Senescent Cell Burden

Senescent cells are living but nonfunctional. All dogs (and people) have some senescent cells, and they do serve a purpose. Specifically, they are associated with wound healing, immune system function, and suppression of cancer.[21] However, as your dog grows older, their senescent cell burden increases, which is a major contributor to aging. You may also recall that senescent cells frequently secrete compounds that recruit other cells to become senescent and further accelerate the aging process. The term for these cells is *senescence-associated secretory phenotype* (SASP). SASP can be measured and used to understand how a person (and ultimately, your doggy) is aging.[22] Supplements and medications that eliminate senescent cells are known as *senolytics*, and as you might expect, a lot of research is going into these. More about reducing your dog's senescent cell burden with senolytics can be found in Chapter 6.

* * *

Diagnostic testing is an incredibly important tool in our quest for longevity for our pets. Most available tests, however, are accessible only through your veterinarian, and the reality is that while the information is valuable, testing alone is not going to make your dog live longer. Our next step is to discuss what you can do now to actually help your dog live a longer, healthier life. Certainly, we will explore high-tech and cutting-edge medicine, but some of the most effective longevity interventions are easy things you can do at home.

PART II

WHAT YOU CAN DO RIGHT NOW

CHAPTER 3

NUTRITION

I've got good news: some of the most effective longevity treatments you can implement for your dog are low-tech and easy to accomplish. When I talk with an owner about how to best care for their dog, regardless of whether the dog is healthy or has a serious medical condition, the discussion always (and I mean *always*) begins with nutrition.

Think of nutrition as you might think of car maintenance. Your car runs on gas, oil, and various other fluids, and it will have optimal performance when the correct fluids are in it. What happens if you use the wrong kinds? Possibly the car will still run, but not as well as it should. It will also be far more prone to internal damage and breakdown. The same is true for a biological system like your dog, except biology is actually much more forgiving than a car.

As simple as it sounds, longevity begins with putting the right fuel in the biological machine that is your pooch. As it turns out, nutrition is actually a big part of the problem—and solution—when it comes to dogs and longevity. When dogs are fed the wrong fuel, over time it causes their bodies to age faster and develop more medical problems than they otherwise would. And because the body takes longer to break down than your car, by the time medical problems are apparent, they have likely been adversely affecting the dog for years and years. Reversing that damage can be difficult and sometimes impossible. This is why, ideally, you should start your pet on an optimal diet from day one, or at least as soon as possible. In this chapter I will outline the most important nutrients, vitamins, and minerals to look for in food; which type of food preparation is best; and the right amount to feed your dog.

FROM WOLVES TO DOGS

When we think about ideal nutrition for dogs, it is best to start with an understanding of where your dog comes from. Depending on what paper you read, dogs have been domesticated for somewhere between 18,000 and 32,000 years.[1] It all started with wolves, *Canis lupus*, who would scavenge the leftovers from our nomadic hunter ancestors. Over a very, very long time, there was an unintentional selection for specific traits in the wolves. The wolves who were less afraid of or less aggressive toward humans and could thrive on their leftover diet became the ones who survived and reproduced. Thus, they created subsequent generations of wolves who were progressively better adapted to living in harmony with people.

The ultimate result of this selection pressure over millennia is the modern dog, *Canis familiaris*. No matter if you own a Chihuahua or Great Dane, they are all the same species. Individual breeds came much later, as they were bred for specific traits to assist in different tasks. The similarities and differences between wolves and dogs are important because they govern what an ideal, longevity-promoting diet looks like.

There are three factors to consider when choosing the best nutrition for your dog:

1. What nutrients are in the food?
2. How are the ingredients processed?
3. How much food is optimal?

(If you are fascinated by this topic and want to learn more details about canine nutrition, as well as the triumphs and failures of the modern pet-food industry, I would refer you to my first book, *The Ultimate Pet Health Guide*.)

1. WHAT NUTRIENTS ARE IN THE FOOD?

There are three sources of dietary energy (calories) in food: *protein*, *fat*, and *carbohydrates*. Literally, that is it; you can't get calories from anything else. Sometimes referred to as *macronutrients*, proteins, fats, and carbohydrates (along with water) provide your dog's body with the raw materials it needs to perform its necessary functions, like building muscle tissue, repairing a broken bone, or maintaining a normal immune system. In addition, micronutrients such as minerals and vitamins are also nutritionally necessary to promote health and longevity. Along with macronutrients, minerals such as calcium, magnesium, and zinc help make up the structure of tissues, while vitamins such as A, B, and C are needed to facilitate normal cellular functions and metabolism within the body.

The big difference between a biological system like your furry friend and an inanimate machine is that biology has an innate healing ability and tendency toward health. In other words, your dog's body wants to be healthy, and given half a chance, it will stay that way. Conversely, if my car is broken, it is going to stay broken until someone (certainly not me!) fixes it. Even if I buy the needed parts for repair and put them next to the car, nothing is going to happen. In a biological system, on the other hand, often all that is needed is the raw materials and frequently the body will take it from there. But for our dogs, we want more than just survival.

When there is a scarcity of one or more nutrients, vitamins, or minerals, the body has to make tough decisions—it has to triage. If you have ever been to a busy human or veterinary emergency room, you have likely experienced triage, with the medical staff prioritizing who is in the most need of care. It turns out a biological system is capable of internal triage.

Have you ever seen a malnourished dog? Of course the dog was shockingly underweight, but there is more to it than that. What did their hair coat look like? What was their energy level and demeanor? When faced with inadequate nutrients, the body has to prioritize, and first on the list is maintaining function of vital organs and the central nervous system. Everything else, like muscle mass, skin and coat, reproductive function, and energy to interact with the environment, takes a back seat. If you have spent time working at a shelter or watch rescue videos online, you have also seen what that dog looks like a few months after being rescued. Suddenly they have better muscle mass and are more interactive. They may even be unrecognizable because their coat is now full and healthy.

Basically, when there is scarcity, the body must plan for today. The prioritization list for micro- and macronutrients is lengthy, and for the body, limiting aging is going to be way, way down on the list; longevity is a future problem.[2] This is the context within which to think about nutrition for longevity. We need to provide the body with enough nutrients not only to maintain critical body function and a normal life span but also to eliminate the need for triage and to ward off the hallmarks of aging.

Protein

When it comes to protein for dogs, the best and most efficient source is meat. While everything your dog eats doesn't have to be animal based, their protein should be. Meat sources can potentially be from just about any animal, although I normally recommend sticking with mammals and birds. In a perfect world, fish would be an excellent protein source, but the oceans are not as clean as we would like them to be, and many fish contain toxins such as mercury and arsenic.[3] The greatest benefit from fish is the fats such as EPA and DHA, which can be supplemented safely by other means—more on this in Chapter 6.

Protein from animal sources can come from muscle meat or organs such as heart, liver, and kidneys. In the United States and other Western cultures, we don't eat a lot of organ meat, but much of the prized nutrition from animals comes from organs, which contain vitamins, minerals, and specific amino acids that may not be found in high quantities in muscle. Most animal predators in the wild eat the organs of their prey first, instinctively knowing where the best nutrition is.

Proteins to sidestep are meat meal and meat by-products. These ingredients are used as a low-cost way to increase the protein content of both kibble and canned diets. They are produced from the leftovers of meat production, and you have no way of knowing what is actually in them, leaving the quality and nutrient content of the protein a complete mystery. Feeding for your dog is about transparency, knowing exactly what fuel you are putting in them. Clearly, meat meal and by-products do not make the cut. The good news is, meal and by-products are easily avoided, as they are listed as such on the ingredients label.

We can't get around the fact that there are some indirect problems to address when considering meat-based proteins. Meat production has a huge environmental impact in terms of greenhouse gases and water and land use.[4] A study from 2017 reported that annual dog- and cat-food consumption was responsible for 64 million tons of greenhouse gases.[5] That's a hard number to ignore. While meat is certainly the most evolutionarily and biologically appropriate protein source for our pets, clearly it comes at a cost, and ultimately, environmental impacts are a longevity issue for all of us.

There is a promising solution on the horizon that allows our pets to "have their meat and eat it too": cultured proteins. Cultured protein is meat that doesn't come from an animal—sort of. The meat is produced from animal cells that are grown, or cultured, to produce meat. There is not an actual cow, pig, or chicken involved in the process, only the cells from one. It sounds a little freaky, but once perfected, cultured meat will have all the nutritional value of traditional meat without the environmental footprint or the need for millions of animals to be farmed. The ecological impact alone will be enormous.

For the time being, cultured meat is still in development. For humans, cultured protein will have to be not only nutritionally correct but also aesthetically pleasing. In other words, it's going to have to look like a T-bone or no one will buy it. Our dogs, however, aren't too hung up on what their food looks like, and pets will be the first big benefactors of environmentally conscious meat protein.

Fats

Fats have multiple roles in your dog's body. They act as a source of stored energy; make up a large part of the skin, cell membranes, and nervous tissue; play a vital role in the absorption of other nutrients; and are involved in a wide array of metabolic processes. Your dog needs dietary fats to survive, thrive, and ensure a long and happy life.

Dietary fats can come from a variety of animal and plant sources. If you are feeding a fresh-food diet, the fat that accompanies the animal protein probably makes up the majority of what they need. And, unlike protein sources for dogs, plant-based fats can still be nutritionally beneficial. Seed or nut oils are commonly used in dog foods. When I designed recipes for dogs in *The Ultimate Pet Health Guide*, plant-based oils were part of most of the recipes.

Naturally, when people think about nutrition for their dog, they tend to transfer what they know (or think they know) about human nutrition, applying it to their choices of dog food. While the ideal nutrient profile for a person is somewhat different from a dog's, a lot of the assumptions people might make about ideal nutrition carry over. When it comes to dietary fats, however, there are two important differences between us and our dogs.

As humans, we are frequently concerned about cholesterol. Diets high in cholesterol can lead to fatty deposits building up in our arteries, which over time can lead to a sudden loss of blood supply to the heart muscle (heart attack) or part of the brain (stroke). This is the reason why people are encouraged to avoid a lot of saturated fats that come from meat in favor of unsaturated fats from plant oils. The great news about your dog is that they don't build up cholesterol in their blood vessels and almost never have heart attacks or strokes. So, your dog can eat saturated fats from meats and not have any ill effects.

The other big difference in fat metabolism between dogs and humans is that of omega-3 fatty acids. Omega-3s are often called essential fatty acids (EFAs) because the body cannot make them and therefore they must come from dietary sources. The most important EFAs are eicosapentaenoic acid (EPA) and docosahexaenoic acid (DHA), which are derived from marine sources such as fish, krill, plankton, and algae. EPA and DHA play vital roles in the body, contributing to nervous system function, eye health, gut health, cardiovascular health, and more. This is why measuring omega fatty acid levels, as discussed in Chapter 2, is so critical to longevity. As humans, we can consume another omega-3, alpha-linolenic acid (ALA), from plant sources such as flax oil or hempseed oil and our bodies will convert the ALA to EPA and, to a lesser extent, DHA. Dogs are largely unable to do this, so their EPA and DHA must originate from marine sources. This is why so many dogs are deficient in omega-3 fatty acids.

But what about toxins? Because supplemental oils like fish oil are a purified product, they can be easily tested by third-party labs for contaminants such as heavy metals and other environmental toxins. Realize, though, that for all supplements there is no legal requirement for products to be tested or the results of the tests to be made public, so in Chapter 6 we'll discuss what to look for in good-quality supplements.

Carbohydrates

Sugars, starches, and cellulose, all of which originate from plants, make up what we call carbohydrates. Carbs provide the body with an energy source (sugar) and, in the case of indigestible carbohydrates, fiber that aids in digestion. Whereas protein and fat are essential nutrients your dog cannot live without, carbohydrates occupy more of a gray zone. Your dog's ancestors evolved eating a diet very high in protein and fat, along with a lesser proportion of carbohydrates. So, while dogs are able to utilize carbohydrates as a nutrient in ways their wolf ancestors cannot, they are not nutritionally required.

For makers of kibble, carbohydrates are a filler and a source of calories that are cheaper than meat. Kibble is basically a baked good, and the common ingredient found in all baked goods—whether we are talking about bread, cake, or kibble—is carbohydrates. You can't make baked goods without a carbohydrate source. Carb sources include grains, legumes (beans), potatoes, and so forth. So, when pet-food companies make the dough that ultimately becomes kibble, they use high levels of carbohydrates to increase nutrient density and ensure the kibble holds together.

Our dogs' ancestors consumed around 6 percent carbohydrates in their diet. The modern dog, who is evolutionarily adapted to a higher-carbohydrate diet, does just fine with a little more, about 15 percent. That "baked good" dry dog food is usually between 45 and 75 percent. Canned food is significantly less, although like kibble it is highly processed—which we will discuss in the "Kibble and Canned Foods" section on page 70—and not optimal nutrition. To be clear, lots of dogs are out there eating high-carbohydrate kibble without any obvious negative effects. While it is true these foods will support your dog's basic needs, these diets are not the optimal fuel for their biological function. High carbs can lead to weight gain, inflammatory conditions such as arthritis, and ultimately a shortened life span. So, a relatively small amount of dietary carbohydrates in the form of fruits, vegetables, and whole grains can be healthy and beneficial. When considering longevity, however, excess carbohydrates are not your dog's friend.

The most visible carbohydrate-related controversy with dog food is the issue of grain-free diets. As mentioned, kibble is high in carbohydrates and frequently uses them as a filler to bulk up the food. In response to pushback on this practice, in the early 2000s pet-food manufacturers started marketing "grain-free" diets. These diets were supposed to be a healthier alternative to foods made with corn, rice, or wheat. Since some kind of carbohydrate has to be used to make kibble, grains were replaced with potatoes, legumes (beans), and other nongrain sources. The problem is, the companies didn't test the foods in a research setting before they started selling them. They merely exchanged one carbohydrate for another.

Some years later, veterinarians started noticing a concerning trend. There was an uptick in a particular type of heart disease in dogs called dilated cardiomyopathy (DCM), which is frequently caused by a deficiency in the amino acid taurine. The increase in DCM was ultimately traced back to many of these grain-free diets.[6] It is still not 100 percent clear if these diets were taurine deficient (as taurine is found in meat and not plant sources) or there was something about them that interfered with the absorption of taurine, but either way the end result was DCM. While the diets in question have mostly now been reformulated to prevent DCM, many people are wary of feeding a diet that is grain-free. But the DCM problem wasn't due to a lack of grains; it was poor diet formulation and a lack of testing. The bottom line here is that dogs do not *need* grains in their diet to be healthy. Many of the fresh, whole-food diets I advocate for do not contain grains, and they are the healthiest diets you can feed your dog.

Water

Clearly, water is an important part of the diet for all living beings. When dogs consume water, they get it from their water bowl or their food. On some level, it doesn't matter that much which bowl it comes from, and dogs are generally good at regulating their water needs. But nutritionally speaking, it is better if the water they consume comes from their food. Maintaining adequate hydration is critical to optimizing function of every system in the body. Even mild dehydration can put stress on the kidneys and affect blood flow, tissue oxygenation, nutrient absorption, and so forth. Every one of the original nine hallmarks of aging is negatively impacted by dehydration.

When a dog is eating a fresh-food diet (more on this in a later section), they are getting a lot of water with every bite they take. Water is necessary in order for food to be properly broken down, as well as aiding digestion and nutrient absorption, so having the water come along with the food is better all around. It may be that the water bowl is right next to your dog's food bowl, but you can't make them drink out of it. In fact, I hear from pet owners all the time, after they switch their dog to a high-water-content diet like fresh food, that their dog barely, if ever, drinks out of the water bowl. You can also add a little water to the food bowl to further increase water consumption. Bottom line: the more water your dog is getting in their food, the better.

There is also the question of water quality. Depending on where you live, your tap water may or may not be clean. We are all familiar with some of the life-threatening water-quality issues that have occurred in places like Flint, Michigan. What you may not be aware of is that tap water in many areas has been shown to be contaminated with pharmaceuticals, agricultural chemicals, and other toxins.[7] Unless you live someplace where the water quality is exceptionally good, you might consider a water-purification system like reverse osmosis because—sorry to say it—those countertop pitchers that filter water just don't make the grade.

Reverse osmosis costs a little money, but this particular upgrade is really as much for the humans in the house as it is for the dogs. It is important for the reverse-osmosis system to have a remineralization feature to replace minerals that are removed during the purification process. Without this, over the long term, reverse-osmosis water can cause a loss of minerals in the body. I've had a reverse-osmosis water purifier under my kitchen sink for years, so all our water for drinking, cooking, and ice is filtered. After you have been drinking properly filtered water for a little while, you become very aware when you drink water that isn't. You can literally taste the difference. I don't know how to describe the flavor of poor-quality water other than that it tastes like chemicals, and it always makes me grateful that I get to go home and drink clean water. As an alternative to reverse osmosis, you could consider bottled water or a water-delivery service, but that can get expensive or be cumbersome. Ultimately, do what works best for you.

Vitamins and Minerals

Vitamins A, B, C, D, E, and K are organic compounds that must be present in the diet in order for normal body functions to be maintained. For example, vitamin A is needed to maintain normal vision, immune system function, and reproductive ability. In the previous chapter, we discussed how most dogs have deficient vitamin D levels and how that impacts the hallmarks of aging. Thinking again of internal triage, if a dog is facing a deficiency, such as a lack of vitamin D, their body has to decide where to allocate what little it has. Vitamin D is a critical part of calcium absorption, and it also reduces inflammation and helps protect the body from cancer. If we consider the body of the severely malnourished dog from before, it will use vitamin D to maintain the biological processes most necessary for life, such as proper immune system function. If vitamin D is deficient to the point where the body can't properly absorb and maintain adequate calcium in the bones, they will lose their strength and rigidity. To be clear, there aren't too many dogs out there who are so deficient in vitamin D that they have the "soft" bones associated with the clinical disease known as rickets. That doesn't mean they aren't deficient at all and might not still be suffering some ill effects such as poor immunity and a greater risk of cancer.

In addition to vitamins, minerals are inorganic compounds such as calcium, potassium, iron, and sodium. Along with protein, fat, carbs, and water, minerals are used to create and maintain every tissue in the body. Mineral deficiencies can lead to all manner of diseases. A lack of potassium, for example, will lead to a loss of muscle strength and coordination and, in severe cases, disturbances of heart rhythm. Magnesium, as we have previously discussed, is associated with accelerated aging and is another frequent deficiency for dogs. In short, vitamins and minerals are critical to maintaining the basic functions of life on a day-to-day basis and promote both life span and health span.

2. HOW ARE THE INGREDIENTS PROCESSED?

When it comes to longevity-focused nutrition, having the proper micro- and macronutrients is critical. But have you considered how those nutrients are prepared and presented to your dog? The basis of food preparation that focuses on health and longevity has everything to do with preserving the nutrition that Mother Nature put in there. In the last section we talked about the importance of proteins, fats, carbs, water, vitamins, and minerals individually, but in reality, that is not how nutrition works. Food sources are not exclusively protein, fat, or vitamins. Animal products, for example, are a combination of protein, fat, vitamins, minerals, and water. Lots of ingredients in one package.

Here is an indisputable fact: every animal species on the planet evolved eating a fresh, whole-foods diet. All their nutrition came from the whole foods they ate. Remember the metaphor of the car and how it is designed to function optimally with specific types of fuel and fluids? When it comes to animals—you and your dog included—we are designed to receive all our micro- and macronutrients through whole foods. The concept of food processing, preservation, and supplements is a human construct designed to provide convenience. There are still benefits associated with appropriate supplementation (see Chapter 6), but in a perfect world, all these vitamins and minerals would be introduced into the body through the whole foods eaten.

Kibble and Canned Foods

You don't need a Ph.D. in nutrition to know that eating more fresh, whole foods and fewer processed foods is healthier. There certainly can be, and are, arguments about ideal diets such as keto, paleo, or vegan, but even at the fringes, no one is advocating for people to improve their health by eating large amounts of processed foods.

In 2020, over $40 billion was spent on pet food in the United States.[8] Of that $40 billion, the sales of fresh-food diets make up only 4 percent.[9] That means that 96 percent of the pet food sold in the United States is kibble and canned. Here's the thing, kibble and canned food primarily exist for one simple reason (and—surprise—it's the same reason processed foods are so prevalent in our diets): our convenience. Kibble and canned diets provide pet owners with a relatively inexpensive food option that won't spoil and has no need for refrigeration. Let me be very clear: no matter what the pet-food companies tell you, highly processed foods like kibble and canned food are not ideal nutrition.

There are two big problems with processed dog foods. For starters, they are manufactured at very high temperature and, in the case of kibble, high pressure. The reason for this is simple: High-temperature and high-pressure processing is necessary if you are going to take fresh ingredients and make them shelf-stable. If you've accidentally overcooked vegetables so long that they turned into grayish-brown mush, beyond being unappetizing, a lot of the nutrition that was originally in those beautiful green veggies has been lost. It is the same with processed dog foods.

Most frequently what is lost are vitamins and other functional compounds such as enzymes. Pet-food companies often add vitamins back to the food after the processing, but the problem is that what is added back may not be as beneficial as what was lost. Naturally occurring vitamins are not so much a single molecule but a complex of phytonutrients. When we supplement a vitamin such as vitamin C, we are adding ascorbic acid, which is a portion of the vitamin C complex rather than the whole thing. As such, supplemented vitamins don't always work as well as those found naturally in whole foods. Additionally, the loss of enzymes or other bioactive compounds is generally not accounted for at all.

The other main issue is what is gained during processing. Specifically, the high temperature and pressure lead to chemical changes in food that have the potential to cause great harm to your dog. Maillard reaction products (MRPs) and advanced glycation end products (AGEs) are formed during the cooking process. In fact, the browning that occurs with cooking is a result of MRP formation. Research has shown MRPs and AGEs contribute to oxidative stress, which causes inflammation, organ disease, and even cancer, affecting most of the hallmarks of aging.[10, 11]

Consumption of MRPs and AGEs in small amounts is probably fine (although less is better) for both humans and dogs. Here's the rub: When researchers evaluated the amount of MRPs in processed pet foods, they found dogs consume 122 times more per day than the average human. The data for AGEs revealed a daily intake 38 times higher than humans.[12] There is no other way to put it—this is not okay.

Frozen, Freeze-Dried, and Fresh

In the grand scheme of things, the best foods to feed your dog for longevity are balanced, fresh, whole foods. There are a few options to try. These days, in pet stores and online you can buy prepared frozen meals that are lightly cooked or raw. Freeze-dried raw diets are great too because the freeze-drying process occurs at low temperature and pressure, so we don't have the nutrient loss and MRP/AGE issue to worry about. These options also have the benefit of a very high water content, assuming you are adding water to the freeze-dried food as directed. Alternatively, you can make food at home. The caveat for home-prepared meals is that it's essential to work from a balanced recipe created by a nutritionist, such as the ones in *The Ultimate Pet Health Guide*. You cannot just put meat and veggies into a bowl and assume your dog is getting everything they need if you want them to live their best and longest life.

3. HOW MUCH FOOD IS OPTIMAL?

After learning that fresh, whole-food diets are a great way to support longevity, a lot of the dog owners I see in my practice are interested in how to implement them. Beyond the inquiries about specific brand or recipe recommendations, the most common question I am asked is, "How much do I feed?"

Consider Calorie Restriction

Research in multiple species indicates that the number of calories consumed per day has a direct impact on longevity.[13] Specifically (although no one really wants to hear this), calorie restriction leads to an increased life span. There are a couple of reasons for this. The first is that calorie restriction upregulates (turns on) metabolic processes like autophagy that have a direct positive impact on the hallmarks of aging. Conversely, higher calorie intake leads to increased body fat, which is associated with inflammation and insulin resistance, both of which promote disease and aging.[14] So, your dog should be eating enough calories to maintain optimal body function and nothing extra.

Both the health and the longevity benefits of calorie restriction are about how *often* your dog eats as much as their daily caloric intake. It turns out that many of the hallmarks of aging are positively affected during periods of not eating, or what is known as intermittent fasting.[15] In dogs, the current research indicates those who eat once daily have "better cognitive function and lower odds of having gastrointestinal, dental, orthopedic, kidney/urinary, and liver/pancreas disorders" compared to those eating more than once daily.[16] To be clear, your dog would need the same amount of food as if they were eating twice daily, just fed in one meal rather than two. The time of day for the single meal is not super critical, although I would suggest an evening meal, as sometimes when dogs are lying down for hours on an empty stomach—as they do overnight—they can get acid reflux and tummyaches. Lastly, the benefits of once-daily eating require your dog to fast between those meals. That means few, if any, treats.

Calculate a Starting Point

I know you're thinking, *This is all very interesting, but* how much *should I feed my dog?* Your starting point should be based on the recommendation for the food you are using. If it is store-bought, the package will have some guidelines. If you are preparing the food, make sure the recipe offers how many calories there are per cup of food. Then you can calculate your dog's daily calorie requirement. The charts on pages 75 and 76 will help you determine your dog's resting energy requirement (RER) and daily energy requirement (DER). Ultimately, DER is the number of calories per day to feed, at least to begin with.

Body Weight (pounds)	Body Weight (kilograms)	RER in kcal/day
2	0.91	65
4	1.82	110
6	2.73	149
8	3.64	184
10	4.55	218
15	6.82	295
20	9.09	366
25	11.36	433
30	13.64	497
35	15.91	558
40	18.18	616
50	22.73	729
60	27.27	835
70	31.82	938
80	36.36	1,037
90	40.91	1,132
100	45.45	1,225
110	50.00	1,316
120	54.55	1,405
130	59.09	1,492
140	63.64	1,577
150	68.18	1,661

Activity	Dog DER
Weight loss	1.0 × RER
Neutered adult (normal activity)	1.6 × RER
Intact adult	1.8 × RER
Light activity	2.0 × RER
Moderate activity	3.0 × RER
Heavy activity	4-8 × RER
Pregnancy (0-42 days)	1.8 × RER
Pregnancy (42+ days)	3.0 × RER
Lactation	4-8 × RER
Puppy (weaning to 4 months)	3.0 × RER
Puppy (4 months to adult size)	2.0 × RER

You should also consider your dog's body condition score (BCS). As shown in the chart on page 77, BCS is evaluated on a 9-point scale, with 5 being ideal. Below 5 is underweight, and above 5 is overweight. Given what we know about calorie restriction and longevity, I recommend shooting for a BCS of between 4.5 and 5. Regardless of whether you are determining the amount to feed from the recommendations on the package or are calculating DER, it is important to aim for your dog's optimal body weight. In other words, if your dog weighs 60 pounds and has a BCS of 6, their optimal body weight is probably closer to 55 or maybe a little less. Calculate the amount to feed based on the weight they *should* be.

1	No visible body fat. Bones visibly protrude from body. Easy to see the pelvis, ribs, and lumbar vertebrae. Emaciated and with clear signs of decreased muscle mass.
2	No tangible body fat when touched. Pelvis, ribs, and lumbar vertebrae all easy to see; other bones slightly visible. Small loss of muscle.
3	Pelvis is beginning to stand out. Tops of lumbar vertebrae are showing. Ribs can be easily felt, with no tangible body fat around them. Prominent abdominal tuck. Prominent waist.
4	Abdominal tuck and waist both easy to see. Ribs can be felt easily, with a small layer of fat covering them.
5	When looking down on a dog, easy to see waist as distinct from ribs. When viewed from side, abdominal tuck is evident. Ribs can be felt even though there is some fat–fat layer is not too thick.
6	When looking down on a dog, waist is visible with some difficulty. Can see abdominal tuck. Ribs can be felt underneath a moderate layer of extra fat.
7	Abdominal tuck may or may not be present, but can no longer see waist when looking down on dog from above. Visible fat buildup where tail meets body, as well as around lumbar area. Ribs can be felt with difficulty under significant amounts of fat.
8	Waist and abdominal tuck are not visible. Stomach and abdomen may be hanging out from the body and look distended. Large fat buildups around lumbar and tail area. Ribs either cannot be felt when touched or are able to be felt only when pressed forcefully. Significant fat covering the ribs.
9	Abdomen is clearly distended. Abdominal tuck and waist are completely missing. Ribs cannot be felt. Huge pockets of fat over the base of the tail, spine, and chest. Fat buildup on individual limbs and the neck.

Any formulas or charts are able to provide you with only a starting point, because regardless of how it is calculated, the recommended daily amount to feed your dog is a guess that hinges on both internal (metabolism) and external (exercise) factors. A friend who is a veterinary internal-medicine specialist once told me that calculating daily calorie requirements for dogs is only something interns do. Here is my "highly scientific" advice: After you calculate a starting point for feeding, keep an eye on your dog's weight and BCS. If they are getting fat, feed them less. If they are getting skinny, feed them more. At the end of the day, it's as simple as that.

PRACTICAL CONSIDERATIONS

Feeding your dog for longevity requires consideration of food ingredients, preparation, amount, and frequency. There is no question that a properly balanced, fresh, whole-food diet fed in the right amount gives your dog the best nutritional advantage for a long and healthy life, and in a vacuum, the chapter ends here. In the real world, however, there are other factors to consider. The biggest challenges pet owners face when it comes to nutrition for their dog (or themselves) are the age-old issues of time and money.

Fresh-food diets necessarily require a commitment of either time or money, although frequently both are involved. Fresh food, regardless of whether it is for humans or dogs, is always going to be more expensive than processed foods. This is why nutrition-related illnesses are so common in people who are economically disadvantaged. Calories from processed foods are cheaper and easier to obtain.

If you own one small to medium dog, the price of pre-made fresh food may be within reach. If you own one or more large dogs, you could easily find yourself spending somewhere north of $500 per month on frozen cooked or raw foods. Let's be honest, for most of us, that is going to be tough to sustain. On the flip side, if you make food at home, there is a time commitment, but you can purchase the individual ingredients yourself and the costs per meal will be significantly lower. In addition, you have control over sourcing ingredients, such as finding a good butcher who can save cuts of meat that are great for dogs but maybe don't sell well for humans. Trimmings from high-quality cuts of meat can be both affordable and nutritious. If organic is within the budget, I highly encourage it. That said, I will choose a conventional fresh-food diet over organic kibble any day.

The bottom line is, whatever you do regarding feeding your dog, you have to go with a plan that is sustainable for your life. If you love spending time in the kitchen, it may be that making food is for you. If you don't even know how to turn on your stove, perhaps not. You can also make as much food as you are able in one go and then portion and freeze. If you can make a couple of weeks' (or more) worth of food all at once, this cuts down your time in the kitchen drastically. There is certainly no need to be doing food prep multiple times per week.

Or you might consider feeding a combination of store-bought fresh food and homemade. And if feeding all fresh food is too much of a financial challenge, feed as much as you can afford and supplement the rest with high-quality canned food or kibble. Read ingredients lists to make sure they contain real meat (not meat meal or by-products). For dry foods, make sure that they are relatively low in carbohydrates. There are also some air-dried kibbles out there that are better than the more conventionally produced kibble. If it is air-dried, you will see it prominently listed on the packaging, as this is a selling point for the company. At the end of the day, we all have to live in the real world, and reconsidering what you feed your dog isn't an all-or-nothing proposition.

One final note regarding diets: variety is a plus. Dogs evolved to eat a spectrum of different proteins, fats, and carbs. Feeding them the same ingredients for years may have detrimental effects, such as the development of food sensitivities. Instead, I highly recommend rotating through different recipes over time. Depending on how sensitive your dog is to dietary changes, you can do this as often as daily or as infrequently as several times per year. If your dog is sensitive to food changes, make sure to gradually transition from one diet to the next over a week or so.

* * *

While nutrition is unquestionably "step one" when it comes to longevity, exercise and lifestyle come in a close second. In the next chapter, we will discover how to build on our foundation of nutrition by exploring ways to create a longevity-promoting environment at home for your furry friends.

CHAPTER 4

EXERCISE AND LIFESTYLE

While optimizing your dog's diet is the foundation for their longevity, providing them with an appropriate amount of exercise and promoting a healthy lifestyle are right up there in terms of importance. The great news about exercise and lifestyle adjustments, compared to just about everything else we discuss in this book, is that they are totally free. Everyone can implement these changes regardless of finances, and when they're done correctly, you will have a huge positive impact on your dog's quality of life and longevity, not to mention your own.

In this chapter we'll explore the benefits of exercise, from better muscle strength and cardiovascular health to improved cognitive function and a more positive emotional state. We'll look at the best kinds of exercise for your dog, as well as how to safely maintain activity in an arthritic dog. We'll also cover your dog's overall lifestyle and where there may be sources of stress that lead to anxiety; what you can do to alleviate it (hint: training can help!); and why it's important to create an environment of stability, safety, structure, and social time.

EXERCISE

For humans, science has been wishy-washy when it comes to what exercise works best for health and longevity. Theories and recommendations come and go. Aerobic exercise was the primary goal for a while. Later those recommendations were replaced with a greater focus on resistance training. Then it was cross-training, then high-intensity interval training—the beat goes on. Through the years, the experts have debated what kind of, and how much, exercise is best for us humans, but the constant they all agree on is that moving our bodies is essential to maintain good health. It's an undeniable fact that an appropriate amount of exercise makes a body stronger and healthier.

Not surprisingly, this is all as true for dogs as it is for humans. We know that a lack of exercise can lead to weight gain (in the form of fat), muscle loss, joint pain, and, in many cases, poor health. That said, too much or the wrong kind of exercise can result in acute injuries, as well as chronic problems like arthritis and back pain and, in turn, poor health. In addition, physical fitness is not necessarily synonymous with longevity. For example, human studies indicate that prolonged aerobic exercise, such as would be seen in marathon runners and long-distance cyclers, can lead to significant heart damage. The same has been shown to be true in laboratory animals.[1]

While I don't have too many patients who are marathon runners or who are signing up for the Tour de France, I do see patients who suffer from the effects of overexercise, and these effects frequently impact a dog's longevity. As you know from the hallmarks of aging, longevity is about a lot more than building strong muscles and maintaining cardiovascular health. We have to consider how exercise is affecting our dogs at a cellular level and then determine the most advantageous types and amounts, rather than focusing only on body fat, muscle mass, and athletic ability. We have all heard stories of extremely fit-looking athletes who get sick and sometimes even die. I've seen this in dogs as well. The truth is, while the longest-lived dogs I have seen are not the sedentary couch potatoes, neither are they necessarily the ones I would have described as athletes. Like everything else when it comes to optimizing health and longevity, exercise is about balance.

Effects of Exercise

When you picture an aging dog, what do you see? What I think of is a dog with decreased mobility, difficulty getting up, pain when moving around, a tendency to slip and fall, and frequently a decline in cognitive function. It's really no different from the signs we expect to see in an aging human. Many, if not all, of these factors relate back to the hallmarks of aging, and regular exercise is one of the tools we have to address and improve bodily processes that lead to a dog being physically old, regardless of their chronological age. But what kind of exercise is best?

Exercise for your dog can take many forms. For most dogs, exercise comes in the form of walks and possibly trips to the dog park. Other dogs get theirs through running, swimming, playing fetch or Frisbee, agility activities, and so forth. Before we examine what types and amounts of movement are most supportive of longevity, we need to start with an understanding of exactly what exercise does within your dog's body.

The effects of exercise on the body can be evaluated on multiple levels, starting with whole-body macro function, as well as drilling down all the way to cellular and subcellular effects, as described in Chapter 1. Beginning with macro effects, dogs who get regular exercise have better muscle strength, cardiovascular health, stamina, balance, and mobility. Studies support our assumptions about improved health due to exercise in that overweight dogs do have a greater risk of death than those of normal body weight.[2] Exercise also has significant positive effects on your dog's mental and emotional state—dogs feel better and tend to maintain a better disposition if they are able to get out and exercise.

One other big-picture piece that may not be as obvious is how exercise affects the cognitive function of older dogs. Exercise's physical and psychological benefits are proven in the oldest humans, as higher exercise capacity is noted as a significant factor in the longevity of people over 100 years old.[3] There is every reason to believe this is the case for our dogs as well. In fact, studies on both animals and humans confirm that regular physical exercise is associated with better cognitive function in geriatric individuals.[4] Declines in cognition are a serious problem in geriatric dogs and frequently manifest as decreased interaction with their owners, wandering aimlessly, walking into corners and "getting stuck," and restlessness and anxiety, particularly at night. Quality of life for both dog and owner becomes a major issue when people aren't sleeping because their dog is pacing and whining throughout the night. In short, exercise equals happier dogs who live longer and have better mental acuity.

Moving deeper into the cellular effects of exercise, research indicates that it has a positive impact on literally every single one of the original nine hallmarks of aging.[5] That's right, all of them. So, yes, exercise will help your dog have more stamina and stay lean and will likely improve their mental state, but the bigger gains occur on a much less visible level. As we continue to shine a light on the various interventions we can undertake to help our dogs live longer and healthier lives, you will find that diet and exercise are the only two to have such a broad impact. Though previously I described optimizing nutrition as the foundation of health and longevity, the truth is that achieving a significant extension of your dog's life span and health span—their quantity and quality of life—requires optimizing nutrition *as well as* exercise and lifestyle.

WHAT IS THE BEST EXERCISE FOR YOUR DOG?

It will come as no surprise to any dog owner that exercise requirements vary from dog to dog. When considering optimal exercise, we need to evaluate who your dog is from the perspective of their breed, as well as their personal tendencies and energy levels.

All dogs like to run and play—it's just that some of them are better equipped to do so than others. Your average dog should be perfectly able to go out for extended exercise sessions, as long as they are conditioned for it. Great exercises for many dogs include walking, running, swimming, and playing with other dogs. Just like us humans, they have to practice and work up to longer or more strenuous activities. Other dogs, however, aren't necessarily designed for that type of exercise. For example, "squished"-face breeds (brachycephalic dogs), such as pugs, bulldogs, and shih tzus, don't always have the best airways, and extended aerobic activity can be difficult for them. Let's just say that going for a five-mile run with your bulldog may not be the best plan. That said, these dogs can do great on long walks. I have a client who regularly hikes for hours with her pug, Pablo. He is super fit and does just fine on these extended outings. Dogs are a lot like people in the sense that they all have their strengths and weaknesses. Some people and some dogs are just built to run; it looks effortless when they do it. Others are more suited for long walks, hiking, swimming, or other activities. Give them options, and your dog will show you what kind of exercise they like.

Beyond physical characteristics, some dogs have a more "active personality" than others. Your average border collie, for example, is a dog who needs a lot of exercise not only for physical reasons but also for mental stimulation. These dogs, along with other herding breeds, are very smart, and in order for them to be happy and calm at home, they need things to do. I frequently tell pet owners that these dogs "need a job." Their job could be learning certain tasks or tricks, obedience training, agility work, and so forth. Usually going out for a long walk with these breeds isn't going to get it done. It's just not enough mental stimulation, and the result can be an anxious, hyperactive, and poorly behaved dog that may or may not tear your house apart when you're not around. If nothing else, exercising your dog appropriately could save you a fortune in replacement and repair costs for chewed-up furniture and door jambs.

One job I like a lot for dogs is nose work: training your dog to find an object using their sense of smell. A dog's sense of smell is between 10,000 and 100,000 times stronger than a human's, and I suspect that to your average dog, smell is as obvious as vision is to us.[6] Nose work is a wonderful mental exercise and a fantastic activity for both high-drive dogs and those whose physical condition may prevent them from participating in more strenuous physical activities.

Put Your Dog's Nose to Work

To begin, you will need a vial containing a small piece of cloth infused with cedar oil or some other aromatic compound. First, have your dog sniff the vial and then reward them with a treat and praise. After they begin to associate the smell in the vial with treats, you can place the vial a little farther away but still in their line of sight. When they come up to it, give them a treat. You can also incorporate a voice cue such as "find" at this stage. Continue this process until your dog begins to look for the vial, even when it is out of sight. At that point, you are off to the races. When you hide the vial, your dog knows it is their job is to go find it. You can hide the vial indoors or in large outdoor areas for an extra challenge.

Related to, but more physically demanding than, nose work is search-and-rescue (SAR) training. This training prepares dogs to assist in finding people lost in the wilderness or urban areas, as well as after disasters. SAR training involves a lot of mental and physical energy on the part of the dog and their handler, as both learn the processes to find and rescue lost people. While many owners go into SAR training specifically to get their dog mission ready for rescues, others do it as a fun activity for both dog and owner. Either way, SAR training can be a fantastic activity for high-drive, high-energy, intelligent dogs and the people who love them.

Another great mental activity for dogs is obedience training. More than just teaching your dog to sit and stick out a paw to shake, obedience can involve dogs learning complex, multistep tasks like navigating a maze or tricks that require patience and real mental focus. The truth about most dogs is that they *want* to give us what we want—we just don't always know how to ask properly. Once you and your dog develop a rapport around training, you can truly accomplish some amazing things.

Regardless of what kind of dog you have, exercise is critically important to their health and longevity. The requisite amount of physical activity and mental stimulation is going to vary from one dog to the next based on their age, breed, size, physical condition, and personal needs. Keep in mind that not every type of exercise is right for every dog or every stage of their life. The goal is to keep them active and engaged (both physically and mentally) to maintain lean body mass and an appropriate weight and provide mental stimulation. The combination of proper nutrition and exercise will help support an ideal body condition score, as we discussed in Chapter 3, as well as have a positive effect on all the hallmarks of aging.

When Exercise Goes Wrong

While exercise inarguably promotes longevity in dogs, as a veterinarian I can't leave this topic until we discuss some of the ways exercise can go wrong. The potential downsides of the wrong types or amounts of exercise begin with a very basic fact about dogs: they live "in the moment." In many ways, a dog's ability to do this is one of their greatest strengths, and it is also one of the greatest lessons we humans can learn from our dogs. Your dog isn't worried about what happened yesterday, and they aren't thinking about what might happen tomorrow. They are in the here and now, and while it is among their most endearing characteristics, there is one problem: when you live purely in the moment, you tend not to consider the consequences of your actions.

Not thinking about consequences can cause all kinds of problems for dogs. A dog might eat a sock that gets stuck in the digestive tract and requires surgery to remove. What will happen if the dog finds another sock the following week? They are just as likely to eat it again. Within the context of exercise, dogs that are running around and playing on a hot day are at risk for overheating and developing heatstroke, which can be life-threatening. They just don't consider the necessity of rest and drinking water. Signs of heatstroke include lethargy, excessive panting, weakness, collapse, and a very dark red tongue and gums. If you notice this happening, get the dog immediately to shade and offer water. You can rinse their feet with cool (not ice-cold) water to help cool them off. Then get them to a veterinarian immediately.

Many dogs will also do things that could cause short- or long-term injuries, because they are out there having fun and not thinking about what might happen. Dogs that play rough or love to fetch are at risk for joint injuries, such as a ruptured cranial cruciate ligament (CCL). The CCL in dogs is the same as the ACL in humans and prevents hyperextension and excessive internal rotation of the knee. Normally, when people damage their ACL, it is because of some kind of traumatic event like a knee hyperextension playing football. In dogs, the damage tends to occur slowly over time. The cruciate ligament gradually becomes strained or slightly torn repeatedly. Eventually, the ligament begins to weaken and tears. Think of it like bending a paperclip in the same place over and over again. Though it has some flexibility, ultimately the paperclip will break from the cumulative strain. CCL damage is the most common orthopedic injury in dogs, and it frequently requires surgery. Dogs with these injuries are prone to arthritis in the affected joint as they get older, which of course will contribute to decreased mobility and difficulty exercising, and subsequently promote aging.

Other than blown cruciate ligaments, the biggest exercise-related problem I see in dogs is the result of high-impact exercise. Consider Frisbee dogs. You have surely seen this, either in person or in a video clip: the dog chases after the Frisbee and leaps to catch it, frequently twisting their body in midair. Admittedly, it looks super cool. In the long term, however, the most arthritic spines I have ever seen are in older dogs who spent a lot of time catching Frisbees. That acrobatic leaping and rotation cause microtrauma to the countless ligaments and tendons that stabilize the spine. Over time, these small injuries compound into calcified soft tissues, a decrease or complete loss of spinal flexion, pain, and lack of mobility. It's a lot like people who were competitive athletes when younger and end up with severe orthopedic or neurologic issues later in life. Regardless of whether the athlete is canine or human, the bill comes due eventually, and the consequences of youthful indiscretions are impossible to ignore later on.

Like so many things in life, the key to safe and effective exercise in dogs is variety and moderation. If your dog loves to catch a Frisbee or chase a ball, I wouldn't want to take that away from them. Since I also want to protect their joints and spine, my suggestion would be to weave in these higher-impact activities with other gentler ones. Maybe take a long walk to a dog park and then throw the ball or Frisbee for a few minutes and then walk home. Now, instead of 30 minutes of constant high-impact activity, you have 10 minutes of high-impact Frisbee and 30 minutes of low-impact walking. This is a great way to keep your dog's mind and body happy.

In the discussion of diagnostic testing in Chapter 2, I mentioned a lab called VDI that looks at a variety of factors associated with aging and injury that are not generally found on the standard blood panel your veterinarian might run. A couple of them can be helpful in both diagnosis of and monitoring treatment efficacy for joint injuries and arthritis—specifically, serum hyaluronic acid (sHA) and C-reactive protein (CRP).

Hyaluronic acid (HA) is the viscous liquid within the joints that provides lubrication. When there is inflammation in one or more joints due to injury or arthritis, HA can leak into the bloodstream. So, sHA is a marker that can be used to measure the level of joint inflammation present in a dog. CRP is more of a measure of inflammation within the entire body. CRP can be elevated for a wide variety of reasons, including infection, autoimmune disease, or inflammation in one or more body tissues, such as joints. A test that combines sHA levels with CRP can provide a window on the level of joint inflammation your dog is experiencing. This can be particularly useful information to determine if highly active dogs are experiencing injuries not apparent just by looking at them. You and your veterinarian can also use these diagnostic tests to measure the effectiveness of treatments to mitigate joint inflammation.*

Maintaining Activity in an Arthritic Dog

In the section above, we discussed how testing from VDI can be helpful in both diagnosis and monitoring of treatment efficacy for joint injuries and arthritis. This can be particularly useful information in dogs whose activity

* There are many options, from Western medicine to holistic alternatives, to treat joint injury, inflammation, and arthritis in dogs. For readers who are interested in a comprehensive deep dive into these options, you will find Chapter 12 of my first book, *The Ultimate Pet Health Guide*, to be filled with details and actionable information.

level is decreased, but it is not clear if this could be due to arthritis. You and your veterinarian can also use these diagnostic tests to measure the effectiveness of treatments to mitigate joint inflammation.

As in arthritic people, it is critical to maintain a healthy level of activity for dogs with arthritis. Their natural tendency is to be less active, so it is important to continue to encourage them to move around. Inactivity leads to decreased muscle mass, which in turn leads to more unstable joints and more joint-related pain. That said, excessive activity, such as jumping or playing too much, can lead to joint inflammation and pain. The key with arthritic dogs is to keep them moving around, even if it is just walking or playing for a few minutes several times daily to maintain or improve their level of function.

LIFESTYLE

Ideally, our goal for our dogs is for them to live an active life full of mental stimulation while being free of stress and anxiety. While even dogs with the best lifestyle are going to have a stressful day from time to time, if stressful days outnumber stress-free ones, it can have devastating consequences.

Everyone has seen and experienced the short-term physical effects of stress and anxiety, such as gastrointestinal upset, changes in appetite and mood, lack of sleep, and so on. All these symptoms hold true for our dogs as well, with stress potentially manifesting as whining, crying, barking, acting frantic, and even destructive behavior. Anything can be a trigger for anxiety, although the most common causes are confinement, being left alone, traveling to new places in cars and airplanes, and being around strange people or animals. Beyond the behavioral issues that occur in the stressful moment, stress also has long-term effects. While this has not been specifically studied in dogs, research into humans with severe mental illness shows a 10-year decrease in life expectancy compared to the average across all people.[7, 8] These impacts are greater than the decreased life expectancy associated with smoking, diabetes, and obesity. Even without severe mental illness, high stress levels in humans have been shown to reduce life span by 2.8 years.[9] The clear correlative is that your dog's mental and emotional state is directly related to their longevity.

Sources of Stress

One of the most common psychological conditions in people is post-traumatic stress disorder (PTSD). This occurs when a person has a stressful or traumatic experience, and the anxiety associated with that experience follows them for months or years after the trauma has ended. The interesting thing is that everyone responds differently to these events. You can look at two people who experienced the same trauma, and one of them is fine while the other cannot shake the fear and anxiety. The differences between these people are thought to be a matter of brain chemistry.[10] Specifically, it is the ability, or inability, of the brain to "forget" traumatic experiences. People whose brains can forget traumatic emotions associated with an event experience less PTSD than those who cannot. When it comes to our dogs, the same is true. Dogs with PTSD may show symptoms similar to those seen in humans, such as "chronic anxiety; hypervigilance; avoidance of certain people, places, or situations; sleep disturbances; fear of being alone; decreased interest in a favorite activity; and aggression."[11]

PTSD is often associated with military personnel, and while that line of work is certainly, and sadly, an all-too-common cause, PTSD can be the result of any kind of trauma. Dogs who have served on military or police forces can develop PTSD alongside their handlers. In fact, the 2015 movie *Max* is based on a true story and follows an ex-military dog with PTSD. Military experiences aside, dogs are sometimes forced to endure some horrible things. Frequently I tell people that any dog who came off the street or out of a shelter probably has some form of PTSD. A lack of food, shelter, and safety are some of the most traumatic experiences a dog (or a human) can have. Similarly, dogs that come out of abusive homes or hoarding situations can also have severe psychological trauma that can manifest in all the same ways as PTSD. Based on their traumatic experiences, these dogs may have specific triggers, such as being aggressive around food or toys, being afraid of people (usually men), or being fearful of specific objects that someone might have used to hurt them, such as a rolled-up newspaper.

Dogs are a lot like humans in that their levels of stress and anxiety are, in part, situational, but they also have their roots in genetics and early cognitive development. We have all seen dogs that are fearful and anxious. While some have faced, or are still facing, legitimately threatening or otherwise stressful experiences, other dogs have never had a bad day in their lives and are still nervous and afraid. Some dogs, like some people, tend to always be on high alert; they are just wired with a tendency to be anxious. These dogs may become fearful in strange situations, around loud noises, in a crowd, when they see other dogs, and so on. They may grow frantic, bark excessively, or try to hide or run away. Fear in these dogs can sometimes manifest as aggression; proceed with caution if you own a nervous dog or if you find yourself around one.

Separation anxiety in dogs is very common and is one of the most prevalent canine behavioral issues. It is estimated to affect one in every four to six dogs.[12] Dogs with separation anxiety panic when they are left alone. Remember, dogs are pack animals, and some of them get nervous when their pack leaves them alone. (And in case you didn't realize it, you and your family are the pack!) Dogs with separation anxiety might whine, bark, become destructive, or try to escape when they are left by themselves. Separation anxiety can have effects on longevity for physiologic reasons such as chronically elevated cortisol levels leading to strain on vital organs such as the heart and liver. In addition, separation anxiety leads to higher levels of owners surrendering their pets to shelters and potentially euthanasia as a result of the dog being un-adoptable.[13, 14]

Whether your anxious dog had a rough start in life that they can't quite shake or they have been a pampered pooch from day one and anxiety just comes naturally, the important thing to note is that high levels of stress can contribute to a shortened life span.

How You Can Help

Mitigating long-term anxiety can be as challenging for dogs as it is for humans. First things first: it's important to realize that you can improve things, but you can't necessarily fix them. I don't mean for this to sound discouraging, because a lot of gains can be made with highly stressed dogs. But the fact is that you are never going to turn an anxious or traumatized dog into the stereotypical golden retriever who loves everyone and is fazed by nothing.

There are three main focuses in alleviating the effects of long-term stress and anxiety:

1. **Secure living arrangement:** Get the dog out of unsafe or uncertain environments to a place where they have a consistent schedule and access to shelter, food, and water.
2. **Training:** The bedrock of helping dogs with anxiety is consistent positive-reinforcement training.
3. **Supplements and medications:** Depending on the circumstances, natural supplements can be beneficial. One such product that has received a lot of attention is CBD. CBD for animals has gained widespread use and acceptance in recent years, and it has long been used to help alleviate stress and anxiety. While CBD is generally safe for dogs, it is best to consult with a knowledgeable source when it comes to product selection and dosing. If your veterinarian is unable to assist, you can find valuable information through the Veterinary Cannabis Society (VCS.pet) and VeterinaryCannabis.org. In addition to natural supplementation, drugs like fluoxetine sometimes work in severe cases of anxiety, but only when used in conjunction with training.

When considering a person with an anxiety disorder, such as a panic disorder, social anxiety, and so forth, you can't simply medicate the problem away. Meds may be helpful, but the real gains are made (1) by ensuring basic needs are met, and (2) through ongoing therapy. For your dog, therapy comes in the form of training. Training provides structure, which in turn gives your dog a sense of stability and certainty.

Dogs thrive on schedules and knowing what to expect from their day. Think about the kinds of things you get stressed-out about—perhaps what your boss is going to say at your next review, how much your tax bill is going to be, or if you are going to find your soulmate. I'd be willing to wager that most or all of the things you are worrying about have roots in some kind of uncertainty. When you or your dog is not obsessing over the unknown, your stress levels are reduced dramatically.

Earlier, we discussed training within the context of mentally stimulating activities, such as nose work, search and rescue, and obedience training. Before a dog can receive more advanced training, they need to begin with the basics, such as "sit," "stay," and "come." Just like a child has to learn their letters before they can read, your dog needs to master the basics before building up to complex activities. Depending on the dog and how good you are with training techniques, the basics can be picked up in a matter of weeks. It takes longer for some dogs than others, and while puppies are always easier to train, you can, in fact, teach an old dog new tricks and lower their stress level in the process.

Training is great for all dogs in that it gives them structure, which in turn helps them feel settled and less stressed. In fact, any kind of training can be beneficial to lower the stress level of a dog. Again, use yourself as an example here. If your mind is occupied with something productive, you are less stressed, right? We tend to get caught up with anxiety when we are sitting around and our minds are idle. Giving your dog things to do and think about takes their mind off whatever is upsetting them. Plus, learning new things provides them with a sense of accomplishment and confidence and offers a chance for you to bond with your pet.

One last thing about training: I highly recommend taking classes or finding an experienced dog trainer to at least get you started. The funny thing about us humans is that we tend to accidentally reinforce the behaviors we are trying to change in our dogs. It stems from the fact that we often approach our dog as if they were a small human, and that approach rarely, if ever, works. Here's an example: A client is in my office with their dog who is barking constantly and generally acting out of control. When the dog begins barking in the exam room, the owner, in an attempt to improve the situation, pets the dog and gives him treats to calm him down. What just happened? The owner "told" the dog that barking and behaving badly gets him rewarded with affection and treats. Despite good intentions, the owner has reinforced the behavior we would like to stop. Instead, the dog should be ignored while he is barking and then get rewarded when he stops. He only has to stop for a second, even just to take a breath, and he gets rewarded. If you do this enough, the dog will begin to associate treats with not barking, and the behavior will improve.

At least 80 percent of dog training is actually people training. More specifically, it is teaching people how to communicate with their dog in a way that the dog will understand. Dogs want to comply with their owners—they want to make us happy. They just don't understand what we want, because we can't seem to communicate effectively on their level. A good trainer or veterinary behaviorist can bridge that gap and help you provide your dog with that sense of security and stability they need to feel safe and calm.

Pack Dynamics

We know that optimal nutrition for dogs is based on the nutrient profile they evolved eating, and the same is true when it comes to lifestyle. Wolves are pack animals, and so are their descendants. This is in contrast to cats, who, with the exception of lions, live solitary lives outside of mating season. Pack animals enjoy being around each other, and they tend to be very social. But socialization in dogs is a learned behavior that should be established from a young age. When puppies are separated from their mother and littermates, usually around eight weeks old, their socialization has only begun. In order to continue them on their path to good behavior, new puppy owners should make sure their pup is getting regular social time with other dogs and people so they learn how to interact. This can be done through a puppy socialization class or by introducing the pup to as many new animals, people, and environments as can be done safely (see discussion on puppy vaccines beginning on page 109). When this doesn't happen, sometimes dogs don't understand how to behave around others, which leads to anxiety, stress, and potentially fear-related aggression.

There is also a natural order, a hierarchy, within a pack—and you are a part of it. In all packs there is a dominant leader known as the alpha. Beyond that, there is a structure where some dogs (or people) are more dominant than others. The tendency of an individual toward dominance is a personality trait that varies from one dog to the next. It is just like how some people are natural-born leaders and will easily take charge of a situation, while others are more comfortable and effective following that leader.

Where you fall in the pack hierarchy has a lot to do with the relationship you have with your dog. In any given household, you, as the human, should be the alpha. As such, your dog will defer to your wishes and be compliant with commands, training, and so forth. When humans don't communicate very well with dogs, sometimes the dog decides they are the alpha, and problems in the house generally ensue. Signs that your dog doesn't see you as the alpha include them not responding to your commands, growling or other aggressive behaviors toward you, or even excessive pulling on the leash when you are out for a walk. If you are dealing with potentially aggressive behaviors, a good trainer is absolutely necessary to help you reestablish yourself as the alpha. If a trainer is not available to you, you could start with online resources or courses. Sophia Yin was a very well-respected veterinary behaviorist who created a lot of available online content through CattleDog Publishing.

A related pack-hierarchy issue that occurs is when, from the dog's perspective, there is no clear alpha in the house, yet the *dog* isn't a natural alpha personality. What happens when you put someone in charge of a large project and leadership isn't their strong suit? There will probably be misunderstandings, a lack of order, and a project that doesn't get done. For dogs, this situation can result in stress, anxiety, and sometimes aggression toward people or other animals because the dog isn't comfortable in the alpha role and, as such, doesn't know how to behave. This is yet another reason why establishing yourself as the alpha in the house provides certainty and stability for anxious dogs.

As pack animals, dogs also look to others for support. For anxious dogs, sometimes having another dog in the house can be beneficial as well. If the other dog has a naturally calm and relaxed personality, the anxious dog will look to the calmer dog for reassurance and key off of their behavior. You would be amazed how much an anxious dog will calm down if they have a calmer dog to look to for guidance.

Ultimately, when it comes to lifestyle, our goal should be to provide our dogs with an environment that offers stability, safety, and structure, as well as social time with other dogs and people. Once that has been established, we have created a foundation for our dogs to live a relatively low-stress life that will promote health and longevity.

HELP YOUR DOG, HELP YOURSELF

As you now know, providing your dog with as close to a stress-free and active lifestyle as possible is paramount to their health and longevity. Positive social interactions with others (dogs and/or humans), coupled with appropriate amounts of exercise, promote a healthy body and mind, and both are necessary to achieve a longer life span for our dogs. The bonus that comes with providing this idyllic, wonderful life for your dog is that you get to live longer too!

When you get your dog out for exercise, you are getting outside as well. This provides you with exercise and likely interaction with other people. The American Heart Association published a retrospective analysis of almost 70 years of scientific studies regarding the health effects of dog ownership.[15] It concluded that dog ownership leads to a 24 percent risk reduction for "all-cause mortality" over an average period of 10 years. This means that, regardless of the cause of death, people who owned dogs had a lower risk of death during the span they were studied than those who didn't. In addition to decreased mortality rates, dog ownership is also associated with improved cognitive and physical function in geriatric adults.[16] Just like with our dogs, a longer life span is only worthwhile when it comes along with good health, and your dog can contribute to that.

Another major benefit of dog ownership is that it makes us happier as people. Trackinghappiness.com surveyed more than 12,000 people and found that pet owners are happier than non–pet owners.[17] (They also found that dog owners are happier than cat owners.) And when scientists evaluated changes in life span associated with happiness, they found that optimistic people have an almost 15 percent increase in life span.[18] So, overall, it would appear that dog ownership creates a synergistic relationship resulting in longevity for both dog and human!

* * *

If you stop reading this book right now, you already have the necessary tools to make a significant improvement in your dog's life span and health span. Optimizing diet, exercise, and lifestyle is the lowest-hanging fruit in our quest for longevity and represents the changes that have the potential to make some of the greatest impacts. They also happen to be some of the easiest and most accessible ones you can make yourself—and they're good for *you* too!

I cannot stress this enough: Whatever you do to promote longevity in your dog, it must occur alongside the triad of optimized diet, exercise, and lifestyle. As we endeavor to help our dogs live longer, better lives, no medical intervention on the horizon will make up for a lack of any one of these things, never mind all three. Ultimately, we are constructing a framework to dramatically extend the life span of our dogs. The first step in any construction project is laying the foundation. It has to be solidly built, or nothing you place on top of it will last. The foundation for longevity is optimizing your dog's body and mind by providing the nutrients, activity, and social interactions they evolved not only to survive but also thrive on. By starting here, we are making sure that the biological machine that is your dog functions to the best of its ability. With that accomplished, we are then free to begin making adjustments to that machine that will result in better performance and an even longer life span, which is what we'll explore in Part III.

PART III

A HOLISTIC APPROACH

CHAPTER 5

UTILIZING ALLOPATHIC MEDICINE

Understanding the mechanics of the processes that lead to aging provides the backdrop for you to be able to take active steps to promote longevity. With the longevity-specific benefits of diet, exercise, and lifestyle now in your arsenal, it's time to look at the kinds of medical care your dog is receiving.

Let's begin with two truths about veterinary medicine. First, all veterinarians practice medicine with the primary goal of taking the best care of their patients. We certainly can, and will, examine some of the ways these good intentions might pave the road to you-know-where, but realize that even when things go wrong, there is no malice or hidden agenda in veterinary practice. I know of no other profession with more sincere, hardworking people than vet med.

The second truth is less optimistic. The pharmaceutical, research, and medical-education community is biased.[1] Medical research costs money (a lot of it), and as such, it is driven toward avenues that optimize potential profits. Universities, which we would like to think are impartial research institutions, function in large part due to grants and endowments from Big Pharma. This relationship sometimes not only leads to a bias in what research is conducted but also may impact the conclusions researchers publish. It will therefore come as no surprise to you that the entire medical system is impartiality challenged.

All doctors, veterinarians and physicians alike, are educated within this murky environment, and our education is extremely parochial. Students are indoctrinated with the message that the only "real" medicine is taught through the institution, and ideas that come from other sources are not to be trusted. As a practical matter, this means veterinary students, and ultimately veterinarians, are instructed not to believe anything that doesn't come from the mainstream medical community—which, as we have just discussed, has a real problem with impartiality.

When you combine these two realities, the product is hardworking and sincere veterinarians with a bias they are likely unaware of and a medical system designed to reinforce that bias by promoting products and procedures that benefit Big Pharma. It makes for a tricky landscape for both veterinarians and dog owners interested in considering other options.

Despite all of this, it bears recognizing the good that Big Pharma does. Many of us would not be alive today without the benefits of vaccines, antibiotics, and modern medical procedures. The average life expectancy for a person in the U.S. today is about 77 years. In 1900, it was 47. One of the most significant factors giving us an extra 30 years of life is improvements in health care. The same is true for our dogs. Yes, the system is flawed and we need to look at it with a somewhat critical eye, but turning our back on allopathic medicine is arguably even more counterproductive than trusting everything the medical system says without question. The best way to leverage allopathic medical care for the purposes of longevity is to take advantage of all the good while sidestepping the practices that either may directly cause harm or could negatively impact aging in the long term. So, let's take a look at what is being recommended and why, including vaccinations, surgical procedures, parasite prevention, dental care, and various drugs.

VACCINATION

The topic of vaccination has become controversial lately, particularly in the age of COVID. In some circles, *vaccine* seems to have become a dirty word. The truth is, vaccines save lives, and if our goal is longevity, protecting our dogs against deadly diseases is a great place to start. However, vaccines can also cause a lot of harm. The key is knowing which to use and when.

There are multiple diseases dogs *can* be vaccinated for, although no dog should be vaccinated for everything under the sun. The decision to vaccinate or not should hinge on five factors:

1. Is there a realistic chance the dog will be exposed to the disease?
2. If the dog gets the disease, how likely is it to do significant harm?
3. Does the dog already have immunity to the disease—in other words, have they already been given a vaccine that confers long-term immunity and therefore don't need a booster?

4. Are there legal or other regulatory requirements for the vaccine?
5. Is your dog going somewhere, such as daycare or a boarding facility, that requires vaccines?

Let's review the various vaccines offered for dogs and consider how to best utilize them to promote longevity.*

Distemper and Parvo

Distemper and parvo are two diseases that can be deadly in puppies. Distemper can be transmitted in utero or by respiratory spread. The symptoms of distemper vary, depending on how old the puppy was when they were exposed. Effects range from respiratory disease to heart and/or brain damage—all of which can be fatal. The virus can also affect the proper formation of teeth in puppies and can cause a thickening of their foot pads; distemper is sometimes also referred to as "hard pad disease." Distemper isn't super common, and when it is seen, it is usually in animal shelters or other environments where large numbers of unvaccinated puppies are housed.

Parvo is a much larger problem than distemper. Canine parvovirus causes severe gastrointestinal disease that includes diarrhea (frequently bloody), vomiting, and a whole host of secondary issues that are frequently fatal if not treated. The big challenge with parvo is that the virus itself is incredibly hardy. Parvovirus spreads through diarrhea from infected dogs and can remain infectious in the environment for up to six months. This means there is a very real chance your dog will come in contact with parvo somewhere. If they are not protected, it could lead to an extremely sick pup.

* For specific detailed descriptions of the diseases that vaccines protect against and vaccine protocols, particularly for puppies, please see Appendix B of *The Ultimate Pet Health Guide*.

Distemper and parvo are commonly combined in vaccines. These combinations may include other diseases, so you may see vaccines called DHPP, DHLPP, DA2PP, or DP. The *D* and one *P* indicate distemper and parvo. The *H* and *A2* refer to canine adenovirus type 1 (CAV1), which can cause hepatitis (H), and canine adenovirus type 2 (CAV2), which can cause respiratory disease. The other *P* is for another respiratory virus, parainfluenza. *L* is for leptospirosis, which is discussed next.

The long and the short of it is that you have to vaccinate puppies for distemper and parvo. If you don't, you are placing them at grave risk of getting a deadly disease. But the other components of these vaccines are up for debate. CAV1 is so uncommon in the U.S. that I would never vaccinate for it; I've never seen a dog with CAV1. Parainfluenza and CAV2 are usually not necessary and are discussed along with bordetella in the section to follow on respiratory viruses. So for puppies in my office, we use DP vaccines exclusively. Be aware that your veterinarian likely does not stock DP vaccines. Most don't. If you are able to source them for your puppy, that is great, but don't worry too much if they have to get a combination like DHPP. Adult dogs frequently don't need to be vaccinated for distemper and parvo, as is discussed later in the chapter.

Leptospirosis

Leptospirosis is a bacterial disease that can cause liver and/or kidney failure. It is transmitted through the urine of infected animals, and most commonly, a dog gets lepto from coming in contact with some kind of contaminated water, such as a puddle, communal water bowl, or things of that nature. Marine mammals such as seals and sea lions can carry leptospirosis as well. If you live near a habitat for these sea creatures, be aware that taking your dog to the beach is also a possible source of infection.

The incidence of lepto varies from location to location, so it is best to check and see how prevalent it is where you live. If you are unsure, you can ask your veterinarian or google "incidence of leptospirosis in dogs map" and look for the most recent publication. My recommendation for dog owners usually hinges on the pet's lifestyle. If the dog is outdoorsy and is off leash at the dog park, nature trails, the beach (in sea-lion country), and so on, a lepto vaccine might be a good idea. If your dog takes walks around the block and then gets back on the couch, you are probably okay without it.

Respiratory Viruses

In certain circumstances, dogs can be exposed to a variety of respiratory viruses, including bordetella, CAV2, parainfluenza, and canine influenza. In the vast majority of cases, these diseases cause relatively mild illness characterized by runny noses and coughing that resolve with minimal or no treatment and thus don't necessarily meet the bar for serious disease. Less commonly, however, they can progress to pneumonia and dangerous health complications.

As a rule, respiratory illnesses are most commonly contracted in enclosed environments where there are a lot of dogs, such as boarding and daycare facilities, so many of these facilities require proof of vaccination for at least bordetella and sometimes influenza. In my practice, I only use bordetella and influenza vaccines when they are required.

Rabies

Rabies is a disease that you absolutely don't want your dog to get. It is 100 percent fatal and is transmissible to humans. Rabies is transmitted through a bite or scratch from an infected animal. The virus propagates in nerves and works its way up to the brain, where it causes fatal brain damage. Dogs with rabies have cognitive abnormalities and may show unprovoked aggression or be mentally dull. The prevalence of rabies varies with geographic location, and rabies vaccination is legally required everywhere in the U.S. and most of the world. Like distemper and parvo, this is a vaccine you need to give at least once when the dog is a puppy. Depending on where you live, there may be legal requirements as to the age at which your dog should be vaccinated, although whenever possible, I like to wait until they are at least six months old. This allows them to get a bit bigger and for their immune system to be more mature. In the U.S., they are required to be vaccinated at one year and then every three years after that.

Beyond the obvious longevity benefits of your dog not getting a deadly disease, rabies vaccination appears to have another, very unexpected benefit. Rabies vaccination has been shown to significantly decrease all-cause mortality in dogs. This refers to any reason a dog might die other than an accident. Rabies vaccination has been shown to reduce the risk of death by 44 percent in dogs ages 4 to 11 months old and 16 percent in dogs 12 months and older.[2] The mechanism of the protective effect of rabies vaccines is unknown, but it does not appear to be directly related to the prevention of rabies.

Lyme Disease

Another vaccine to consider is for Lyme disease. As you may be aware, Lyme is a tick-borne disease, and in certain parts of the U.S., such as the Northeast, it is very common. Lyme can lead to autoimmune disease, affecting the joints and central nervous system. While dogs with Lyme cannot transmit the disease directly to humans, we can get it from the same ticks that infect our dogs. Not all dogs with Lyme will have symptoms, and the ones that do frequently will develop joint inflammation and pain. In humans, however, the illness can be devastating and cause issues ranging from joint pain to chronic fatigue and autoimmune disease. Lyme can be treated with antibiotics, although the infection cannot always be cleared, and in cases where the immune system is involved, problems often persist even after the organism has been eliminated. Vaccination for Lyme disease should be based on how prevalent the disease is in your area. You can ask your veterinarian about prevalence or google "incidence of Lyme in dogs map" and look at the most recent map.

Rattlesnake Vaccine

One last vaccine to mention is the rattlesnake vaccine. I know it sounds a little weird, as clearly a vaccine is not going to prevent a rattlesnake from biting your dog. Instead, it can decrease the effects of rattlesnake venom. *It is important to note that any dog with a suspected snakebite needs to have immediate medical attention, regardless of vaccination status.* If you live where rattlesnakes are prevalent and your dog spends time off leash, you may want to consider this vaccine. Rattlesnake vaccines are initially given as a series of two followed by a booster every 6 to 12 months, depending on the level of potential exposure to rattlesnakes.

Of all the vaccines mentioned here, however, this one has the highest probability of an adverse reaction, such as lethargy, vomiting, diarrhea, hives, and so forth. Usually, these are not life-threatening, but I recommend this vaccine only if you feel there is a significant chance of your dog going head-to-head with a snake. In these circumstances, I also highly recommend rattlesnake-aversion training, which teaches dogs to run away if they hear that distinctive rattle.

How Do Vaccines Work?

Vaccines, by design, cause inflammation, which stimulates the immune system and creates antibodies that are prepared to attack the disease in question should the dog be exposed. We've already discussed the impacts that inflammation has on longevity, so it stands to reason we would like to limit the amount and duration of inflammation in the body. The first step in limiting vaccine-induced inflammation is to not give too many vaccines at the same time. Ideally, dogs should be given no more than one at a time, and allowing a month between necessary vaccines is a good idea. In larger dogs, you might be able to get away with doing two on the same day, but if it is at all avoidable, spread them out.

One important fact the vaccine manufacturers won't tell you is that most vaccines last far longer than what it says on the label. This is particularly true for distemper, parvo, and rabies. In my experience, dogs that were properly vaccinated as puppies usually will carry immunity to all three of these diseases for a lifetime without subsequent boosters.

Just like with all aspects of health care, the most effective approach to vaccines is treating each dog as an individual. Immunity to distemper, parvo, and rabies can be checked with a vaccine titer. A titer measures the antibody levels in your dog's blood to see if they have adequate immunity to a given disease. I will normally titer dogs for distemper and parvo at one year and again at four years of age. If they come back low, I will revaccinate, but this doesn't happen often. If they have a good titer at four years old, there is no need to ever retest or revaccinate again. In 25 years of practice, I have never seen an adult dog that was properly vaccinated as a puppy get distemper or parvo. Not once.

Rabies titers are a little more complicated. The process works exactly like a titer for distemper or parvo except that there is a legal issue to consider. As I mentioned previously, rabies vaccines are required by law. Even though they have been shown to last far longer than their label suggests, a titer demonstrating immunity to rabies is not legally acceptable as a substitute for vaccination.[3] There isn't really any medical justification for this; it's simply the way the laws are written. While you can do a rabies titer on your dog and not vaccinate them, you are operating outside the law and are liable if your dog should bite or scratch someone. In addition to this being financially devastating, your local animal-control jurisdiction has the right to quarantine, and even potentially euthanize, a dog if they are a rabies suspect. Be aware of the risks to both you and your dog.

What Should I Be Concerned About?

When it comes to vaccines, there are two specific concerns: The first is a vaccine reaction. This is an allergic hypersensitivity to one or more of the components in a given vaccine. Symptoms can include facial swelling, hives, vomiting, and diarrhea. In rare cases, a life-threatening reaction called anaphylaxis causes a drop in blood pressure and restricts breathing. To the pharmaceutical industry's credit, the quality of vaccines has dramatically improved in the last 20 years, and vaccine reactions these days are rare. When I first started out as a veterinarian, we used to see at least one or two reactions per week. Now, it's almost never. This is due partially to most veterinarians giving fewer vaccines and partially to higher-quality vaccines.

The other concern is a little vaguer but potentially more dangerous. The vaccine inflammatory response can be achieved by a number of methods, including using modified, noninfectious live virus in the vaccine or using killed virus along with inflammatory compounds known as adjuvants. Adjuvants frequently contain metals such as mercury or aluminum. While it is unknown if the adjuvants in vaccines will cause problems in any individual dog, the best policy is to avoid them if possible. DP vaccines are available as modified live but other vaccines such as rabies and leptospirosis are only available as killed, adjuvanted vaccines. This is one more reason why dogs should only be vaccinated for severe diseases they have a reasonable chance of being exposed to. Less is more.

It is possible for the immune-stimulating effect of vaccines to lead to the formation of autoantibodies that can attack your dog's own cells, a process known as *vaccinosis*.[4] This has been documented in both humans and dogs. In humans, it can result in severe diseases, such as rheumatoid arthritis and Guillain-Barré syndrome. In dogs, causality is difficult to establish because the onset of autoimmune disease is frequently months after vaccination. Although we can't definitively connect autoimmune disease to vaccines, they could be implicated in severe conditions like autoimmune hemolytic anemia and thrombocytopenia, among others. There are also reports of neurologic disorders being associated with vaccination.

Pet Insurance

Within the chapters of this book, a lot of discussion focuses on preventive care and promoting longevity through keeping pets healthy. All of this is critically important information. We do have to recognize that at some point your pet will get sick or possibly injured. When that occurs, the medical care necessary to restore your furry family member back to health is likely to get expensive. These days, emergency care for a very sick pet can climb into the tens of thousands of dollars quickly. Unlike human health care, there is no social safety net to guarantee treatment for the uninsured. More often than not, the end result of a pet with a curable condition whose owner cannot afford treatment is euthanasia. This is, without question, the most heartbreaking experience a pet owner or veterinarian can have.

When people find themselves in these situations, there are options. They can put the charge on a credit card or apply for credit through a service specifically designed for medical care, such as CareCredit. Please realize, your veterinarian is unlikely to be able to help with the costs. Veterinary medicine, like it or not, is a business that has to pay its employees, the expenses for drugs and supplies, rent, and so forth. I've owned veterinary hospitals for 20 years, and believe me, if we can help, we will.

But if we routinely discounted or waived fees when people had financial hardships, we would go out of business.

The solution to all of this is pet insurance. I recommend pet insurance to every new client and for every new pet I see. Pet insurance can help defray some of the most expensive medical bills for animals. As is the case with human insurance, there are variables such as deductibles, exclusions for preexisting conditions (no Obamacare for pets), coverage limits, and so on. There are also some policies that cover alternative care, such as acupuncture and other holistic or complementary therapies. I strongly recommend thinking about what you want out of a policy. In other words, do you want a low deductible and higher premiums, or vice versa? Then do some Internet research and look at the policies offered by the many companies out there and read online reviews of those you are considering. The best plan is to obtain pet insurance early, before your pet has any significant medical history. This way, there will be no concerns about preexisting conditions that are not covered.

I cannot stress enough the degree to which pet insurance saves lives and allows for better care. From a longevity perspective, securing a good policy for your pet is one of the most impactful things you can do to support their health.

SPAY AND NEUTER

The term *spay* most commonly refers to a surgical procedure called an ovariohysterectomy in which the ovaries and uterus of a female dog are removed. *Neuter*, also known as an orchiectomy or castration, is when the testicles of a male dog are removed. These procedures are performed routinely in dogs across the U.S. for population control, to decrease behavioral problems, and to a lesser extent for medical reasons. We will focus on the latter two for our discussion of longevity.

Behavioral Issues

Behavioral issues are a real concern for some dogs. Aggression toward other animals or people can lead to injuries and sometimes death. When dogs have significant aggression issues, there is a greater likelihood the dog will be euthanized as a matter of safety or because no one is willing to accept the liability of having a potentially dangerous dog in their house. We can all agree that dogs with aggression issues are a problem, and any veterinarian will tell you they have had to euthanize a healthy dog for these reasons. But does spaying or neutering decrease aggressive behavior?

The veterinary establishment will answer this question with a resounding yes. And many people in the dog-breeding, training, and behaviorist world may say the same. So, it might come as a surprise that the research demonstrates the opposite. It shows a slight increase in aggression and fearfulness toward strangers (people or dogs) in dogs that are spayed or neutered.[5] Interestingly, this difference is only significant for dogs that were spayed or neutered at a young age, between 7 and 12 months. There was no difference in aggression for intact dogs compared to those spayed or neutered after 12 months. This suggests that a dog's brain development, and their subsequent reaction to strangers, is affected by their hormones during puberty. The tendency among veterinarians and trainers to blame behavioral problems on dogs being intact likely stems from long-held beliefs within the profession and the reality that a subset of people who chose to not spay or neuter their dogs tend to be less likely to train them properly and/or may even encourage aggressive behavior. The take-home message here is that fearful and aggressive behavior in dogs is related to early spay and neuter but is also influenced by training and a stable home environment. You can decide if you want to spay or neuter your dog, but you should wait until they are at least 12 months old.

Medical Issues

If you ask a veterinarian why they recommend spaying or neutering your dog, one of the reasons they will cite is that it is better for their health. Certainly in female dogs, concerns about mammary tumors (breast cancer) and pyometra (a life-threatening uterine infection) are legitimate. In male dogs, it is a little less clear. When they get older, intact males can develop a testicular tumor or benign prostatic enlargement. These are less immediately life-threatening than mammary tumors and pyometra but are still something to be aware of. The bigger question is, what is the difference in life span between dogs who have been spayed or neutered and those who have not?

Looking at this from an all-cause mortality perspective, research shows that spayed and neutered dogs have an increased life span of 26.3 percent and 13.8 percent, respectively.[6] So, on average, sterilized dogs live longer. If we dig a little deeper, however, we find that intact dogs are more likely to die from trauma, infectious disease, cardiovascular disease, and degenerative diseases such as arthritis. Sterilized dogs, by comparison, are more likely to die from cancer and immune-mediated disease. Let's consider the relative preventability of these causes of death. Of the primary causes of death for intact dogs noted by the study in question, certainly trauma is avoidable. Most infectious diseases the study evaluated (parvo, distemper, heartworm, and parasitic diseases) are preventable. Cardiovascular disease isn't really preventable, but arthritis can be helped through appropriate exercise and supplements. Cancer and immune-mediated disease, the main causes of death noted for sterilized dogs, are much, much tougher to control for. While there are many ways we can mitigate the risk of cancer and immune disease (which we will discuss), preventing trauma and infection is much easier.

Another study that evaluated age of spay or neuter relative to the incidence of certain types of cancer, hip and elbow dysplasia, and knee ligament injuries found that Labrador retrievers, golden retrievers, and German shepherds had higher incidences of all these conditions when spayed or neutered prior to one year of age.[7] Since this study focused on age of spay or neuter, there is still a question as to whether the benefits of remaining intact diminish after the dog is fully physically mature. In other words, spaying or neutering after dogs are fully grown may not impact their health one way or the other.

There are some surgical options that kind of split the difference regarding spay and neuter. One is a surgical procedure called an ovary-sparing spay, where the uterus is removed. This keeps female dogs hormonally intact, as they still have their ovaries, so presumably they retain the benefits of not being spayed while eliminating the possibility of pyometra as well as an unexpected pregnancy. Male dogs can be vasectomized, meaning the cord that delivers sperm from the testicles through the urethra during mating is cut. Thus, the dog cannot reproduce but still maintains his source of sex hormones such as testosterone. Ovary-sparing spay and vasectomy can be an attractive option for dog owners feeling a lot of pressure from others to sterilize their dog, although once the dog is physically mature, it is unclear if there are ongoing advantages to maintaining their ovaries or testicles. Some general practitioners offer these procedures, but most veterinarians do not have the training for it. If no general practitioner is available, a veterinary surgical specialist will be able to provide these services.

The decision to spay or neuter your dog is multifactorial and includes health concerns, behavioral concerns, and a generous helping of social responsibility and societal pressure. For some reason, people want to judge others for keeping their dog intact. Many people feel owners of intact dogs are irresponsible due to the perceived (but not actual) increase in aggressive behavior and concern for unintended breeding. Looking through the lens of longevity, my recommendation would be to at least wait until they are fully physically mature prior to going to surgery. For most dogs, that means when they are 12 to 18 months old, although giant breeds such as Great Danes, mastiffs, and so forth can continue to grow beyond two years old. If you understand the relative risks and benefits of not spaying or neutering at all and can handle the potentially derogatory comments from folks at the dog park, you might consider holding off altogether.

PARASITE PREVENTION

Routine parasite prevention to consider for most dogs includes heartworm disease, gastrointestinal parasites, and fleas and ticks. There is absolutely a place for these kinds of preventives within the scope of longevity medicine. Like everything else, the most advantageous use of these medications depends on your individual dog's situation.

Heartworm Disease

Of all the parasites dogs can get, heartworms unquestionably have the deadliest consequences. The disease is exactly what it sounds like: your dog gets worms that live in their heart (as well as their lungs and blood vessels). Heartworm disease leads to heart and lung damage and, if untreated, is fatal. In fact, the treatment for heartworm disease in and of itself can be fatal, so proper prevention is critical.

Heartworms are transmitted by mosquitoes. When a mosquito infected with heartworm bites your dog, it leaves behind larval heartworms, who get to work on becoming adult worms. Within a couple of months, these worms take up residence in the bloodstream, heart, lungs, and blood vessels and begin to cause damage over a period of years.

Heartworm prevention involves giving your dog a drug called ivermectin or a similar drug in the same class. Products such as Heartgard and Interceptor utilize ivermectin and are labeled to be given monthly to prevent the larval-stage heartworms from maturing into adult worms. But ivermectin is not necessarily a completely benign drug. Some breeds, such as collies, may have a gene mutation called MDR1 that can make them sensitive to ivermectin and thus more susceptible to side effects, including vomiting, diarrhea, and neurologic problems—which in rare circumstances can be fatal. It should be noted that the dose of ivermectin present in heartworm preventives is low enough that even MDR1-positive dogs are usually fine. It is also easy to test your dog for MDR1, either through your veterinarian or with an over-the-counter genetic test like Wisdom Panel or Embark (see Chapter 2).

There is another possible side effect of ivermectin. The drug is antibacterial and has been shown to cause changes in the microbiome in both animals and humans.[8] As we have already discussed, gut health is intimately associated with whole-body health and longevity. Though you're probably aware that indiscriminate use of antibiotics is a bad idea for gut health, you may not realize that a monthly dose of heartworm preventive could be having similar effects that might include GI upset or medical conditions associated with immune system imbalance.[9, 10]

When we take a hard look at the cost-benefit analysis of heartworm preventive versus heartworm infection, we first have to consider environmental factors. Is heartworm disease prevalent where you live? This is mostly a factor of climate and the presence of mosquitoes. Warmer, more humid climates like the southeastern portions of the U.S. have very high rates of heartworm disease. Where I live on the West Coast, rates are much lower because the climate is more temperate and drier, thus fewer mosquitoes. Interestingly, the areas of higher incidence of heartworm disease are spreading on the map, most likely due to the overall climate getting warmer. The American Heartworm Society maintains maps of the incidence of heartworm disease across the country that you can find on their website.[11]

Depending on where you live and how outdoorsy your dog is, you may have some options regarding heartworm prevention. If you live in a place where the incidence of heartworm disease is very high—Texas, Alabama, Florida, and so forth—you need to keep your dog on heartworm preventive year-round because it never really gets cold enough to kill all the mosquitoes. In climates where there is a real winter, you may be able to take a few months off the preventive during the cold months when there are no mosquitoes. This will at least allow your dog's body and biome a chance to recover from whatever changes the ivermectin has caused. In yet other areas where there are no mosquitoes, you may be in a position to not put dogs on heartworm preventive at all.

The decision about when and how to use heartworm preventive is one to take seriously. If people choose to not use it year-round, their dog must have a heartworm test every 6 to 12 months to make sure they have not been exposed. Also, if your dog should test positive for heartworm disease, the necessary treatment will be much, much more dangerous to them than the preventive ever could have been. Within the discussion of longevity, skipping heartworm prevention at times of minimal risk is ideal, but if there is any question about potential exposure, use the preventive! In this case, it is the lesser of two evils.

Gastrointestinal Parasites

Gastrointestinal parasites include a variety of worms (gross!) such as roundworms, hookworms, whipworms, and tapeworms. Dogs can also get microbial parasites like giardia and coccidia. It isn't important to cover the specifics of each of these infections other than to say it is better if your dog doesn't have parasites.

Most parasites are contracted through fecal-oral transmission, meaning your dog was nosing around poop or someplace on the ground where poop had been, and they ingested parasite eggs. The one notable exception to this is tapeworms, which are contracted when your dog eats a flea. Most parasites are easily treated with medication. This is one of those times when a pharmaceutical is the best solution, since treatment is usually quick and effective. It is always a good idea to run a stool test annually to make sure your dog is clear of parasites. If you live somewhere warm and humid, consider testing every six months.

Fleas and Ticks

Fleas and ticks are a different story than heartworm disease or gastrointestinal parasites. Fleas, in general, are largely a nuisance more than anything else. In warm and humid climates, severe flea infestations can be life-threatening, but this is rare and usually only occurs in very small or very sick animals. As mentioned, fleas can also transmit tapeworms, but these are easily treatable and do not generally cause serious disease.

The good news about flea-control methods is that you can use them as needed. If there are a lot of fleas out there, use a preventive. If the weather outside is cold enough, you can probably skip it. Remember: it is never winter inside your house. If you have a population of fleas reproducing in your home, you've got some work to do.

Ticks are more problematic than fleas, because they can transmit diseases such as Lyme, ehrlichiosis, and anaplasmosis, among others. Interestingly, tick-borne diseases such as these do not always cause visible illness in dogs. Chronic infection, however, can set up long-term inflammation and potentially trigger autoimmune disease, both of which are definitely not conducive to a long and healthy life. Another thing to remember about tick control is that it is not only about your dog's health. As discussed earlier, Lyme is an absolutely devastating disease in humans, and if your dogs are bringing ticks home, you are at risk as well.

Unlike with heartworm preventives, there are a lot of options out there when it comes to flea and tick control. They include orally administered products, topicals, collars, and sprays. Each has its pros and cons when it comes to efficacy and impact on longevity, and oral tick control products are the most commonly recommended by veterinarians. They are good at killing fleas and ticks, although the flea or tick has to bite the dog in order to be exposed to the drug and subsequently die. There are some concerns with oral meds. They are all in the same class of drugs known as isoxazolines, which potentially cause muscle tremors, ataxia (loss of balance), and seizures in some dogs. In my experience, these side effects are rare and short-lived, but they do happen. When it comes to long-term side effects, the truth is, we really don't know, because determining causality related to long-term medications is very difficult unless a specific disease is implicated.

Topical products and flea collars both repel and kill the fleas and ticks, so they offer the benefit of not necessitating a bite in order for the flea or tick to be exposed and die. In addition to your dog avoiding getting bitten, it also means they are less likely to carry insects/arachnids home that could get on you and your furniture. The flip side, of course, is that topical flea and tick products are chemicals on your dog's coat that you will come into contact with. In both humans and dogs, exposure can cause rare side effects like skin irritation, gastrointestinal upset, and potentially even neurologic complications.

The other flea-and-tick option for your dog is natural sprays, usually composed of essential oils. When used as directed, these products are very safe. They are effective at repelling, and even potentially killing, fleas and ticks, although they will never be as dramatically effective as their pharmaceutical cousins. Natural sprays can be a great option when the fleas and ticks aren't too bad. You can google "flea and tick incidence map" to see what your area is like, although if you have had your dog for any period of time, you probably already know from experience. Choosing what kind of prevention to use is a cost-benefit analysis hinging on the amount of exposure your dog has to fleas and ticks. When it comes to orals or topicals, just remember that less is more.

DENTAL CARE

Just as your dentist is constantly reminding you, dental health is critically important to overall health, and that applies to dogs too. Evidence in both dogs and humans shows that good dental hygiene is correlated with a longer life span.[12, 13]

Good dental health for your dog starts at home. Regular tooth brushing, ideally daily, is the single best thing you can do to keep your dog's teeth healthy and supportive of longevity. Depending on the size of your dog, you can get a dog-specific toothbrush or a small toothbrush meant for people. Toothpaste for dogs is mostly about flavor in order to make the experience interesting—that can be really useful for a dog who doesn't like the brush in their mouth! When you brush, concentrate your efforts along the gumline and outer surfaces of the teeth since that is where most issues occur. You will have to train your dog to accept tooth brushing, just like with anything else. Start slowly and be very gentle. If it hurts, they aren't going to give you a second chance. Whether you can brush every day or not, you might consider supplementing with raw bones, dental chews, oral rinses, and so forth. A raw bone—something you can buy refrigerated or frozen—given weekly can be a great way to keep your dog's teeth clean. The goal is to get a bone small enough for your dog to chew through. It will clean their teeth as they are chewing it, and because it is raw, it is fully digestible. When it comes to chews and rinses, I strongly encourage you to use only all-natural products. We want to limit your dog's environmental toxin exposure, and giving them dental treats with antibacterial chemicals is not ideal.

Regardless of how diligent you are with oral hygiene at home, your dog is going to need their teeth professionally cleaned from time to time. In my office, we like to augment home dental care with periodic nonanesthetic dental cleanings. These procedures do not take the place of a full cleaning under anesthesia, but they can help with spots you are missing with your home care. Nonanesthetic dentals should only be performed in veterinary offices under the direct supervision of a veterinarian. It is quite common to find dental problems during these procedures that necessitate a consultation, dental X-rays, and a full cleaning under anesthesia.

What to Do When Your Dog Resists Tooth Brushing

Unquestionably, tooth brushing is the "gold standard" for keeping your dog's teeth clean. But let's be honest, sometimes tooth brushing is easier said than done. We are all busy people, and not everyone is able to set aside the time for regular tooth brushing for their pet. Not to mention that it's not necessarily the favorite pastime of our dogs either!

While some dental home care is going to be better than none, we do need to consider the best alternative options outside of brushing (please keep trying). Dental chews, oral rinses, and additives to your dog's water bowl can all be helpful. Since dental care is an ongoing, lifelong process, however, we must consider the potential long-term effects of dental-care products. Many such products for animals contain chemicals like chlorhexidine and sodium hexametaphosphate. While there is no definitive evidence of negative long-term health impacts associated with these compounds, my preference is to "keep it natural" whenever possible. There are natural dental-care products on the market for dogs that utilize algae, enzymes, curcumin, and other ingredients that will help keep teeth clean when used regularly. Products such as these are a great addition to your dog's home dental-care plan. That said, please try to brush as often as possible.

ANTIBIOTICS

As a class of drugs, antibiotics are unquestionably life-saving, and many of us (and our dogs) would not be alive today if not for access to drugs to control bacterial infections. And a major reason for the extra three decades of life humans enjoy on average today is that we rarely die of bacterial diseases.

So, I am not debating the efficacy and usefulness of antibiotics—but they can also lead to serious problems. The most direct concern is what these medications are doing to the microbiome. So what happens when you disrupt the normal gut flora through the use of antibiotics? It depends both on the duration of the course of antibiotics and on the age of the human or dog taking the medication. In humans, long-term use of antibiotics in older patients is associated with increased all-cause mortality.[14] While we don't have the same studies in dogs, it is reasonable to suspect that disruption in the gut biome is going to have negative impacts similar to those seen in humans.

Antibiotics are prescribed far too liberally in veterinary medicine. In many cases, oral antibiotics are used for conditions that can be treated in other ways, such as minor skin infections, or for diseases that don't respond to antibiotics, such as viral infections. The allopathic paradigm is to use antibiotics as if they don't have any negative side effects. As an integrative practitioner, I do sometimes prescribe antibiotics for my patients. However, I always begin by looking for an alternative, and if I have to use antibiotics, I make sure to put the dog on a prebiotic and probiotics during and for at least 30 days after the course of medication, as dysbiosis, or an imbalance in the microbiome, can have both short- and long-term effects, including diarrhea, vomiting, and more systemic immune system imbalance. If your veterinarian wants to put your dog on antibiotics, respectfully ask if there is another option or if it is okay to try something else first. There are going to be times when antibiotics are a necessity, but in many cases, other options may be available. The bottom line: use antibiotics if they are absolutely necessary, but avoid them whenever possible.

NSAIDS

Nonsteroidal anti-inflammatory drugs (NSAIDs) are among the most commonly used pharmaceuticals in veterinary medicine. As a human, you have probably taken your share of ibuprofen (Advil), naproxen (Aleve), and so on. They work well for preventing discomfort caused by inflammation, such as arthritis, muscle soreness, back pain, and so on. If you have a dog with arthritis or back problems, you are likely familiar with NSAIDs. But like any drugs, they can also cause problems. While they are tolerated well by most dogs, NSAIDs are known to potentially cause GI upset, stomach ulceration, and potentially liver and/or kidney problems. Most of these complications are experienced in the short term—days or weeks after starting use. It is, however, good practice to monitor liver and kidney function with a blood test at least annually for dogs on these medications. NSAIDs should be used only when needed and at the lowest effective dose.

Other long-term side effects of NSAIDs that could affect longevity are unknown. Some laboratory studies even show a positive effect on longevity with NSAID use, although we can't immediately assume that what happens in yeast and fruit flies will also happen in our dogs.[15, 16] Even though we don't know if long-term use causes problems, the best practice is to utilize natural anti-inflammatories and pain-relieving herbs, such as curcumin and boswellia, as long as they are able to keep your dog comfortable. You will usually know this by monitoring their activity level, although there are blood tests available to gauge markers of inflammation such as hyaluronic acid levels run by VDI Laboratory. Keep NSAIDs to a minimum. That said, if using them gives your dog a better quality of life, then by all means do so. (You can learn more about how to treat dogs' pain and inflammation holistically in Chapter 12 of *The Ultimate Pet Health Guide*.)

IMMUNOMODULATING DRUGS

Immunomodulating drugs comprise medications such as prednisone, cyclosporine, and others. These drugs are sometimes used for serious medical conditions such as cancer and autoimmune disease, and in these cases, they can be lifesaving. They are also often prescribed for less serious issues, like allergies. These are strong pharmaceuticals and should be reserved for serious medical conditions. (Chapter 11 of *The Ultimate Pet Health Guide* discusses allergies in detail, along with ways to control them without immunomodulating pharmaceuticals.)

As the name would imply, these drugs affect the function of the immune system. More specifically, they suppress the immune system. Since we know how important the immune system is to overall health and the prevention of infections and cancer, you can see why it would be best not to intentionally decrease immune system efficacy. Like any other veterinary decision, the choice has to be made based on the specific medical condition of your dog, and there are cases where immunomodulating drugs are the best course of action. Whenever possible, however, they are best avoided or kept to a minimum.

* * *

When used appropriately, allopathic medicine is highly beneficial and promotes longevity. The problem, of course, is Western medicine tends to overuse these methods because they are the only tools in the toolbox. As with everything in life, balance is the key to success, and the most advantageous way to utilize allopathic medicine to promote longevity is by balancing its use with natural supplements.

CHAPTER 6

SUPPLEMENTS

Supplements are any substance taken to provide extra nutrients to augment your dog's diet. Ideally, they come from natural sources, although in some cases they can be synthetically created. Supplements come in different forms: capsule, tablet, powder, or liquid. I talk with a lot of people about which supplements are right for their dog, and the key to supplementation for longevity is to keep an eye on which of the hallmarks of aging any given supplement addresses and create a regimen that addresses as many as possible.

Since frequently the patients I see have serious medical conditions, like cancer, organ failure, and autoimmune disease, the strategy for supplementation hinges on how to best address what is going on with the individual dog. When it comes to general longevity, however, there are a core set of supplements that almost every dog will benefit from. Beyond that, the individualized nature of medicine comes into play.

If you google "supplements for longevity," you will receive about 17 million hits—I just tried it. Even if you could snap your fingers and instantly eliminate all the redundancy and general Internet garbage, you would still be left with an incredibly long list of supplements that have legitimate positive effects on longevity. So how are you supposed to know which ones are best to give your dog? In this chapter I will outline my recommended supplements, explain how they can have a positive effect on the hallmarks of aging, and discuss whether they should be taken periodically or long term.

THE AMAZING VERSATILITY OF SUPPLEMENTS

Countless times in my career I have seen a dog for a chronic problem that allopathic medicine has not been able to resolve. Whether it is arthritis, cancer, gastrointestinal disease, skin issues, or anything else, it's really a question of providing the pet with something their body needs to help it heal itself.

Oftentimes with healthy animals you don't see dramatic changes when you begin supplementation because, largely, we are trying to maintain their level of good health. With sick pets, though, the improvements can be surprising.

I see many dogs and cats whose owners and veterinarians have exhausted the conventional therapy options for arthritis, and their pet is still in pain. Sometimes, the medications these pets can take are limited due to concerns about side effects, such as kidney, liver, or gastrointestinal complications. Utilizing natural anti-inflammatory and pain-relieving supplements—for example, boswellia, curcumin, fish oil, and others—can make a life-changing difference in these animals. Not only do supplements such as these have positive impacts all on their own, but they can also almost always be used in conjunction with pharmaceuticals—and they even have the ability to mitigate some of the side effects of the pharmaceuticals, such as protecting liver function.

SUPPLEMENT OPTIONS

The 30-plus supplements presented in this chapter are my top picks for availability, safety, and effectiveness, according to the information we have right now. They are used regularly for people interested in their own longevity, and while many are not commonly given to dogs, they are safe at the dosages noted. (Even so, I always recommend consulting with your veterinarian before starting any supplement or medication for your dog.) Plenty of other supplements out there successfully promote longevity, so there's no way this could be a complete list, but it is a great place to start. Plus, now that you are familiar with the hallmarks of aging, you will know what to look for when you encounter something not on this list.

Given the lack of regulation in the supplement industry, it can be a challenge for pet owners to source high-quality supplements. As consumers, we all must do our due diligence when choosing supplements for our pets . . . and ourselves. When it comes to pet-specific supplements, the National Animal Supplement Council (NASC) is an organization that evaluates supplements to make sure they are made well and contain what they say they contain. You can be sure products with the NASC seal are high quality. For pet products that don't have the NASC seal or supplements made for people, the best strategy is to do some research, look for reputable brands, and, when possible, get a brand recommendation from someone with knowledge about the supplement in question.

The following supplements are categorized alphabetically and then presented in a chart, noting which of the original nine hallmarks of aging they help counter. Keep in mind that anything you plan to do for the sake of your dog's longevity has to be sustainable on your end, otherwise it is likely not going to be an effective long-term strategy. At the end of the chapter, we will discuss supplement strategies to obtain the best results while keeping in mind your commitment of time and effort.

Please note that you will not be giving your dog every single one of these supplements included in this chapter—I will offer advice on how to choose a few to focus on to promote your dog's longevity. Let's get started!

Ashwagandha

Withania somnifera, also known as ashwagandha, is an herb whose uses in traditional Indian medicine date back as far as 6000 B.C. Ashwagandha has long been used to promote longevity, and now with the benefit of modern scientific research, we understand why.

Ashwagandha is described as an *adaptogen*, or an herb that helps the body manage stress. More specifically, ashwagandha enhances telomerase activity, lengthening those important telomeres that protect chromosomes from damage.[1]

It also addresses deregulated nutrient sensing by increasing AMPK and inhibiting mTOR, the proteins that help balance the body's response to food.[2, 3]

Dosing of ashwagandha varies depending on how the herb is processed. For unprocessed, granulated ashwagandha, give 1 to 10 grams twice daily, depending on the size of your dog. For extracted and dried preparations, give 0.25 to 2.5 grams twice daily. As a liquid extract, 1 to 5 milliliters can be given twice daily.

Berberine

Berberine is another herb that has been used in various forms of traditional medicine for thousands of years. It occurs in many plants, including goldenseal, Oregon grape, and barberry, among others. Berberine has positive effects on longevity through AMPK activation and by suppressing senescent cells—cells that, due to damage, no longer function properly—so that they don't negatively affect working cells.[4, 5]

Since berberine is a constituent of other herbs, there isn't a specific dosing level to give. You can give extracts of various berberine-containing herbs (where the levels of berberine will vary) and also products sold with concentrated berberine. For dogs, the best source is an herbal extract (liquid, powder, or capsule) of a berberine-containing herb that is made for dogs. Berberine is generally safe, and the most common side effect is GI upset.

Carotenoids

Carotenoids are a class of compounds produced by plants that are yellow, orange, and red. These are what give many fruits and vegetables their bright colors. Carotenoids such as beta-carotene (a vitamin A precursor), lycopene, lutein, astaxanthin, zeaxanthin, and so forth are potent antioxidants and, when part of a dietary and supplement regimen, have an effect on improving immune function,[6] as well as limiting genomic instability and certain types of cancer.[7]

Carotenoids are found in pet foods, although probably not in quantities sufficient to promote longevity in our dogs. As noted, there are a lot of carotenoids out there, and you don't have to supplement them all. The better plan would be to use a supplement containing multiple carotenoids and/or rotating through different ones over time. Dosing recommendations here are a little tricky, since it depends on which carotenoids you are considering. For example, I use astaxanthin at a dose of 2 to 8 milligrams per day, depending on the size of the dog, to help with skin and coat, as well as overall inflammation levels. Similarly, you can use 10 to 20 milligrams of lycopene and 500 to 2,000 IU of beta-carotene per day.

CoQ10

Coenzyme Q10 (CoQ10), also known as ubiquinone, is naturally present in all animals and most bacteria. CoQ10 is an antioxidant and anti-inflammatory, and it plays a role in cellular energy generation. It has been shown to help control diabetes and improve cardiovascular, liver, and kidney function.[8] CoQ10 specifically supports mitochondrial function (providing energy to cells) and genomic stability (accurate replication of DNA), both combating important hallmarks of aging.[9]

CoQ10 is not water-soluble, which means it has to be given with a fatty meal or in a preparation that specifically makes it more absorbable. A good dosage for dogs is between 10 and 100 milligrams per day for a small dog and large dog, respectively.

Curcumin

If you are familiar at all with supplements for dogs or humans, you are probably aware of curcumin. This yellow pigment is the active ingredient in the herb turmeric, and it possesses antioxidant, anti-inflammatory, and liver-protective properties. Interestingly, it also has properties that can reverse stem cell exhaustion and prevent genomic instability. In other words, curcumin can make older stem cells act younger[10, 11] and prevent errors in DNA replication.[12]

Curcumin is not particularly well absorbed by the GI tract, so simply feeding your dog (or yourself) turmeric will not have much effect. The absorption of curcumin can be increased by combining it with fat and black pepper, but even then, it still isn't great. Successful supplementation with curcumin requires the use of a preparation specifically designed to be more bioavailable. This is frequently done by a process called microencapsulation, which makes the curcumin water-soluble and thus easily absorbable. Appropriate dosing of curcumin is highly dependent on the way it is produced, as different encapsulation processes have different effects. In this case, I would suggest finding a high-quality, highly absorbable product. If the product is for dogs, follow the dosing instructions. If it is for humans, give one-quarter of the recommended dose for small dogs and the full adult human dose for large dogs. You can give your dog this supplement every day.

EGCG

Epigallocatechin gallate (EGCG) is the component in green tea that makes it so good for you. EGCG is anti-inflammatory, and it has been shown to protect the brain and the heart. As a pro-longevity supplement, EGCG mitigates cellular senescence, mitochondrial dysfunction, epigenetic alterations, and deregulated nutrient sensing.[13, 14, 15, 16] Dose at 100 milligrams for a small dog and up to 750 milligrams for a larger dog.

Essential Fatty Acids

In Chapter 2, we discussed the pro-longevity benefits of EPA and DHA, the essential fatty acids found in fish oil. The almost five-year increase in life span for people consuming fish oil is due to its effects on multiple hallmarks of aging, including reducing telomere attrition, mitochondrial dysfunction, deregulated nutrient sensing, and altered intercellular communication.[17, 18, 19, 20] If you are concerned about fish oil for environmental or other reasons, you can find supplements made from marine algae. Another essential fatty acid, alpha-linolenic acid (ALA), is found in nuts, seeds, and their associated oils. While ALA is not converted to EPA and DHA in dogs as it is in humans, it has its own benefits, including suppressing genomic instability and mitochondrial dysfunction.[21, 22, 23]

There is a wide range of dosing recommendations for essential fatty acids. For the purposes of longevity, a good dose to start with would be about 250 milligrams of combined EPA and DHA for a small dog and up to 3,000 milligrams for a very large dog. For ALA, use 20 to 200 milligrams per day for small and large dogs, respectively. Omega-3 fatty acid levels can and should be measured in dogs (see Chapter 2). This will allow you to really know if your dog is getting enough essential fatty acids. The goal is to supplement so they test at the upper end of what is considered normal.

Fisetin

Fisetin is a compound found in various fruits and vegetables, such as strawberries, apples, persimmons, and cucumbers. Fisetin has been found to be a potent senolytic, meaning it can rid the body of senescent cells.[24] The dose of fisetin is between 20 and 150 milligrams for small and larger dogs, respectively, and it should be used around two to three days per month to allow the body to "clean up" excessive senescent cells.

Magnesium

Magnesium came up in Chapter 2 during the discussion of diagnostic tests. This mineral plays a role in boosting energy metabolism and cell proliferation, while slowing apoptosis (programmed cell death), oxidative stress, and inflammation.[25] Magnesium is found in dark leafy greens, nuts, seeds, beans, and grains—depending on the food you give your dog, they may be getting enough magnesium in their diet.

Magnesium can be supplemented orally, although it has a tendency to cause GI upset. My suggestion is to use it topically by rubbing a magnesium cream into bare skin for absorption. Since your dog may already be getting enough magnesium, hold off on supplementing magnesium until they are tested. Once you know their levels, you will know how much to supplement.

Melatonin

You might be familiar with melatonin as a supplement used as a sleep aid. Melatonin is also an antioxidant, and it has been shown to prevent cellular senescence. Interestingly, melatonin is produced in the gastrointestinal tract in response to intermittent fasting, which we already know has positive effects on longevity. There has been some speculation that one of the benefits of intermittent fasting is the production of melatonin, and it is possible that supplementing with melatonin may have similar effects.[26, 27] Melatonin is very safe and can be dosed between 0.5 and 5 milligrams per day, depending on the size of your dog.

Mushrooms

Mushrooms are ubiquitous around the world and truly illustrate what people mean when they say "food as medicine." Mushrooms are known to have properties that help fight cancer, support the immune system, promote recycling of old cells (autophagy) and thus limit senescent cells, and the list goes on.[28] A recent study showed mushroom consumption in people decreased overall mortality during the study period by 16 percent.[29] Among the most powerful medicinal and longevity-promoting mushrooms are ganoderma (reishi), shiitake, chaga, turkey tail, and cordyceps, although there are many more. Some of these can be consumed as food, and some require their active ingredients to be extracted in alcohol or hot water or by other means.

Dosing of mushrooms for longevity varies based on the type of mushroom and/or the nature of the extract. The good news is that at the end of the day, mushrooms are food, so they are very safe. If using a product made for animals, follow the directions. If you are using a human product, use one-quarter of the recommended dose for small dogs and a full adult dose for larger dogs.

N-Acetylcysteine

N-acetylcysteine (NAC) is derived from the amino acid cysteine and has several therapeutic uses in human and veterinary medicine, including helping break up mucus in the lungs and also treating toxicities such as acetaminophen (Tylenol) overdose. As a longevity-promoting supplement, NAC has been shown to help reduce oxidative stress as well as address genomic instability and mitochondrial dysfunction.[30, 31] NAC can be dosed in dogs between 100 and 400 milligrams twice daily for small and large dogs, respectively.

NMN

Nicotinamide mononucleotide (NMN) is a precursor to nicotinamide adenine dinucleotide (NAD). NAD is a critical component of all cells in the body and plays a role in energy generation and cellular repair. NAD is thought to decrease the inflammation that accompanies and promotes aging (inflammaging).[32]

Since NAD is not effective when given orally, its precursor, NMN, is the next best option. There is research evidence to suggest that NMN can reverse age-related conditions through stimulating the production of NAD.[33] NMN supplementation can be dosed between 50 and 500 milligrams per day for small dogs and large dogs, respectively.

Oleuropein Aglycone

Oleuropein aglycone is derived from olive oil and olive leaves. This fascinating compound has received a lot of attention for its potential benefits for people with Alzheimer's disease and dementia. It promotes cellular autophagy and thus helps the body rid itself of senescent and other damaged cells, as well as supporting proteostasis (the process that recycles misfolded proteins).[34, 35] It also prevents oxidative damage and has anti-inflammatory effects.

Products containing oleuropein aglycone are usually powdered olive leaves or olive leaf extract. For powdered olive leaves, give about ¼ teaspoon in food per day for small dogs and 1½ teaspoons for a large dog. Alternatively, give between 5 and 75 milligrams of an extract that contains at least 12 percent oleuropein.

Plasmalogens

Every cell in the body has a membrane that creates the boundary between inside and outside the cell. The cell membrane is largely made up of molecules called phospholipids, along with various receptors and channels within the membrane that allow for transfer of materials, cell signaling, and so forth. Plasmalogens are a form of phospholipid that occurs in all mammalian cell membranes, although it is found in the highest concentrations in the brain, red blood cells, and muscle tissue.[36] Plasmalogens appear to serve a critical purpose as antioxidants, and higher levels of plasmalogens are associated with neurotransmitter release, longevity, decreased inflammation, and improved cognitive function. They may also have value in the treatment of neurodegenerative diseases.[37, 38]

Plasmalogens show a lot of promise in the field of longevity medicine, although there have been no studies looking at their use in dogs. That said, plasmalogen supplementation is safe and something you might want to consider if you have an aging dog, especially if there is some concern about their cognitive function. One of the most prominent researchers in the field of plasmalogen supplementation is Dr. Dayan Goodenowe, and you can purchase supplements through his website, www.prodrome.com. The supplements are not inexpensive, so only use them if you feel your dog really needs them. There isn't a known dose for dogs, and I would recommend giving them one-quarter of the adult human dose for small dogs and as much as a full human dose for dogs over 80 pounds.

Probiotics

Most of us are familiar with probiotics, which contain bacteria that are beneficial for gut health. The gut contains approximately 70 percent of the immune cells in the body, so gut health directly translates to overall health and longevity. An unhealthy microbiome is so detrimental to overall health that it is specifically labeled as one of the hallmarks of aging. In addition to protecting us from infections, cancer, and so forth, the immune system controls the body's level of inflammation, which is a factor in two of the original nine hallmarks of aging: cellular senescence and altered intercellular communication. The term *inflammaging* specifically describes how chronic inflammation promotes the aging process. Thus, it will come as no surprise that a healthier gut will help protect your dog from the effects of aging.

Without question, a healthier gut starts with nutrition in the form of a balanced, fresh, whole-food diet. The correct nutrients feed beneficial gut bacteria and limit the harmful ones. We can further improve these effects by utilizing probiotics for gut health, and research confirms probiotics play a role in limiting inflammation and aging.[39] Their potency is generally measured in "colony-forming units," or CFUs. Good-quality probiotics should report CFUs per serving in the billions. Other beneficial additions to probiotics are prebiotics (food for beneficial bacteria) and postbiotics (the beneficial components created by these bacteria). Pre- and postbiotics are sometimes added to probiotic supplements.

If your dog is eating a balanced, fresh, whole-food diet, they are likely getting enough prebiotics. Postbiotics are fatty acids such as medium-chain triglycerides found in some fats like coconut oil. A small amount of coconut oil can be added to your dog's diet—between ⅛ and ½ teaspoon per day, depending on the size of the dog. Dosing of probiotics is highly variable, depending on the product and the health status of your dog. There are strains of probiotics that are specifically for dogs, but you can use a human product as well. You can certainly use a dog or human product off the shelf and see how it works, although you may be able to get some guidance from your veterinarian on how to select a formula right for your dog.

Pterostilbene

The class of compounds called polyphenols is commonly found in fruits, vegetables, teas, and spices. These micronutrients frequently have antioxidant properties.

Pterostilbene is one such compound, and it is the main antioxidant component of blueberries. Pterostilbene has been shown to limit oxidative stress, inflammation, and aging in research models.[40] In addition, there is evidence it can play a role in the prevention and treatment of age-related cognitive decline, which is definitely an issue for some older dogs.[41] Within the scope of the hallmarks of aging, pterostilbene promotes proteostasis.[42] Misfolded proteins not only are nonfunctional but also can be a cause of significant disease and aging, so being able to refold or reuse these proteins has immense benefits. Dosing of pterostilbene for a small dog would be between 25 and 50 milligrams per day and between 100 to 150 milligrams for a larger dog.

Pycnogenol

Created from the bark of the French maritime pine tree, pycnogenol is a standardized extract that contains multiple flavonoids. These compounds are extracted from all kinds of plants and have natural antioxidant activity. They have been shown to play a role in longevity through limiting inflammation, reducing oxidative stress, promoting circulation by keeping blood vessels healthy, and maintaining cognitive function.[43, 44, 45, 46] Anecdotally, pycnogenol has been reported to help dogs with conditions ranging from allergies to arthritis and even cancer. Pycnogenol can be given to dogs at a dose of 20 to 100 milligrams per day for small and large dogs, respectively.

Quercetin

Quercetin is a flavonoid, like pycnogenol, and it possesses many of the same properties that keep the body healthy and promote longevity.[47] And quercetin has additional effects: it promotes proteostasis[48] and may help reduce senescent cell burden.[49, 50] In longevity-specific research, quercetin is frequently used along with the drug dasatinib to reduce senescent cell load. Dasatinib is a chemotherapy drug used to treat leukemia (see Chapter 7). Quercetin can be given to dogs at a dose of 250 milligrams per pound once daily on an empty stomach.

Resveratrol

Resveratrol is one of the more well-known longevity supplements. It is the main component of grape-seed extract, which has long been used to promote health and longevity. Resveratrol is a polyphenol and has many of the same positive effects previously discussed with regard to pterostilbene.[51] Resveratrol has also been shown to promote longevity through positive effects on multiple hallmarks of aging by regulating oxidative stress, energy metabolism, nutrient sensing, epigenetics, and apoptosis, and by improving mitochondrial dysfunction.[52, 53] As you can see, resveratrol can be a big player in the field of longevity supplements.

The active form of resveratrol is trans-resveratrol, and dosing should be determined by the trans-resveratrol content of a given supplement. Dosing is 100 to 500 milligrams per day, depending on the size of the dog.

Selenium

Selenium is an essential micronutrient that is a component of enzymes and proteins in the body that help with the production of DNA and prevent cell damage and genomic instability.[54, 55] Like every other mineral we have discussed in this chapter, not having enough selenium in the body can be detrimental.

One particular fact to note about selenium is that too much is equally bad, and since selenium is usually dosed in very small amounts (micrograms), it is best to avoid using standalone selenium supplements, as there is a risk of toxicity. I strongly recommend supplementing only using a multivitamin that contains selenium. If you use a product made for animals, follow the directions on the label. If you are using a human supplement, consult with your veterinarian or a veterinary nutritionist for guidance.

Serine

Serine is an amino acid that is used by the body to create proteins, and like almost all amino acids, it occurs in both an L form and a D form. In the case of serine, both forms have positive effects on longevity, although from a supplementation perspective, we are focusing on L-serine. Serine is thought to regulate proteostasis and cellular senescence.[56] Serine is also neuroprotective, and there is evidence to support serine's use as a treatment for neurologic diseases such as ALS in humans.[57] Degenerative myelopathy in dogs is very similar to ALS, which provides hope of a treatment to improve quality and quantity of life for dogs with this otherwise untreatable disease. Serine may also improve learning, memory, and immune system function.

For longevity purposes, a good dose of serine should be about 0.5 milligrams per pound of body weight. For dogs with neurologic diseases, and specifically degenerative myelopathy, the dose is much higher. In humans with ALS, doses of 15 to 30 grams (yes, grams) of L-serine per day had a positive effect.[58] For dogs, give 1 gram for a small dog and 10 grams for a large dog.

Spermidine

It's not what it sounds like . . . sort of. Spermidine is a chemical compound found in plants such as soybeans, vegetables, and grains. Yes, it is also found in semen, but spermidine supplements are solely derived from plants, such as wheat-germ extract. (The germ is the reproductive part of the plant.) Setting aside the strange name, spermidine has been shown to extend life and have antiaging effects in laboratory animals and humans.[59] It improves mitochondrial function and proteostasis, induces autophagy, and acts as an anti-inflammatory and antioxidant.[60] Dose spermidine at 0.5 milligrams once daily for small dogs and up to 1 milligram once daily for large dogs.

Sulforaphane

Sulforaphane is a compound derived from cruciferous vegetables such as broccoli. Research shows it affects genomic instability, deregulated nutrient sensing, proteostasis, and mitochondrial function. It also has antioxidant and anti-inflammatory effects, as well as anticancer activity.[61, 62] Dosing of sulforaphane is in the range of 10 milligrams for small dogs and up to 20 milligrams for large dogs.

Vitamin A

The longevity effects of vitamin A are discussed in the "Carotenoids" section on page 139. There is no longevity-specific dose for vitamin A, but dosing of 2,000 IU per pound of body weight has been shown to be safe, although probably higher than necessary. Consider 500 to 2,000 IU per day based on the size of your dog.[63] Note that vitamin A is fat-soluble and should be given with food.

Vitamin B

There are eight different types of B vitamins, and while we don't need to get into a detailed discussion of each, you should realize the scope of cellular and metabolic processes that are regulated in part by B vitamins. This family of vitamins plays a role in energy metabolism; DNA methylation, synthesis, and repair; and immune system function. Not surprisingly, deficiency in one or more of these vitamins can lead to problems, including dysfunction of mitochondria and the immune system, as well as inflammatory diseases and cognitive decline.[64] Two of the B vitamins, cobalamin (B_{12}) and folate, can be easily measured through a blood sample.

B vitamins are naturally found in foods like meat, liver and other organ meats, leafy greens, and so forth. Supplementation of B vitamins for dogs is best done using an appropriately dosed multivitamin or B-complex preparation. If you get one made for dogs, use the dose recommended on the label. B vitamins are water-soluble and you really can't do much harm, but you can certainly combine them with other vitamins, such as A and D. If you are using a multivitamin for humans, consult with your veterinarian or a veterinary nutritionist.

Vitamin C

Vitamin C is another vitamin with a wide range of antiaging effects. It limits oxidative stress, genomic instability, and telomere attrition, as well as modulating senescent cells and inflammaging.[65, 66] Intravenous vitamin C in high doses is also used by integrative and functional medicine practitioners for the treatment of cancer patients. Like the B vitamins, vitamin C is water-soluble and, other than the potential for gastrointestinal upset, there are no realistic concerns about overdosing. Natural sources of vitamin C consist of a wide variety of fruits and vegetables, including citrus, bell peppers, tomatoes, broccoli, and so forth.

Vitamin C can be supplemented in many different forms such as ascorbic acid, Ester-C, liposomal vitamin C, vitamin C with rosehips, and so forth. The dosing will vary depending on the type of supplement being used. The most common form of vitamin C is ascorbic acid, and the dose of that ranges from 250 milligrams per day for small dogs and up to 1,000 milligrams per day for very large dogs. Doses can be split twice daily, which may limit the chance of GI upset if your dog has a sensitive tummy. For other forms of vitamin C, use the dose recommended for products made for animals, or consult with your veterinarian or a veterinary nutritionist if using a product made for humans.

Vitamin D

One of the major functions of vitamin D is the regulation of calcium and phosphorus in the body. Low levels of vitamin D can lead to decreased calcium absorption. In humans, this is a contributing factor to osteoporosis, a weakening and fragility of the bones. While we don't see this phenomenon in dogs, vitamin D also plays a role in the prevention of sarcopenia, or loss of muscle tissue.[67] Poor muscle mass is something commonly encountered in older dogs, and it can contribute significantly to deteriorating quality of life as a result of decreased mobility and joint pain. Vitamin D also helps regulate immune system function and prevent cancer.[68, 69] From a hallmarks-of-aging perspective, vitamin D can aid in maintaining telomere length and in intercellular communication.[70, 71]

Dogs do not make their own vitamin D from sunlight like we humans do, and in my experience, many dogs are deficient (see more about this in Chapter 2). Since both age-related sarcopenia and cancer are widespread among dogs, vitamin D is absolutely something that should be monitored and, when needed, supplemented. The amount of vitamin D to supplement is dependent on blood levels, so get your dog tested. It is possible to overdose vitamin D, so blindly supplementing is not recommended, although the amount of vitamin D found in a multivitamin for dogs is fine. Symptoms of vitamin D overdose include a buildup of calcium that may lead to kidney damage and/or the formation of calcium-based kidney or bladder stones. Vitamin D is a fat-soluble vitamin, so it should be given with food.

Vitamin E

Vitamin E is an antioxidant and anti-inflammatory, and may lower the risk of cancer.[72] Vitamin E also reduces mitochondrial dysfunction, enhances cognitive performance, and can improve signs of arthritis in dogs.[73, 74, 75]

Natural sources of vitamin E include nuts, seeds, and leafy greens. Vitamin E can also be given within a multivitamin made for dogs. If using a multivitamin for humans, check with your veterinarian or a veterinary nutritionist for a specific dose. As a standalone supplement, vitamin E, generally in the form of alpha-tocopherol, can be dosed in the range of 100 IU per day for small dogs and up to 400 IU per day for large dogs. Vitamin E is fat-soluble, so it should be given with food.

Vitamin K

There are two forms of Vitamin K: K_1, which plays a role in blood clotting, and K_2, which impacts calcium transport and deposition in the bones.[76] Both K vitamins affect aging and longevity by limiting the senescent cell burden through promoting apoptosis, modulating inflammation and oxidative stress, and preventing mitochondrial dysfunction.[77] They also have anticancer properties and, along with vitamin D, help regulate calcium within the body.[78]

There is generally no need to supplement vitamin K_1, assuming your dog is eating a properly balanced diet. But if you are supplementing vitamin D, you should also add vitamin K_2, and there are supplements that contain both. K_2 comes in two forms: MK-4 and MK-7. MK-7 is the preferred choice, at a dose of around 20 to 40 micrograms per day along with vitamin D. As vitamins K and D are both fat-soluble, administer with food for best absorption. If using a multivitamin for dogs, give the recommended dose. If using a multivitamin for humans, consult your veterinarian or a veterinary nutritionist for the right dose.

Zinc

Zinc is a micronutrient that has wide-ranging effects with regard to longevity. Zinc promotes immune system function, limits oxidative stress and inflammaging, and prevents mitochondrial dysfunction.[79, 80] While there is a syndrome in dogs called zinc-responsive dermatosis that results from a deficiency, most dogs will get the zinc they need from a well-balanced diet. For supplementation, use a dose of about 1 milligram per pound per day.

SUPPLEMENTATION STRATEGIES

Longevity is, by definition, a long-term practice. You don't have to—and probably shouldn't—give your dog everything all at once. Rotating through and alternating supplements is an excellent way to obtain the biggest benefits while not having to give too much at any one time. In addition, certain supplements are good for the long term, while others should be on a periodic rotation. The ideal scenario is to add your dog's supplements to their food whenever possible, because giving long-term supplements orally is often not sustainable.

Long Term

First on the shortlist for long-term supplementation are probiotics. The bottom line here is that gut health is the cornerstone of immune system health and whole-body health. There may be benefits in periodically rotating through different probiotics to give your dog's body a variety of bacteria, but having them on some kind of probiotic for the long term is recommended.

Omega-3 fatty acids, like EPA, DHA, and ALA, are also great long-term additions to support longevity. I highly recommend supplementing EPA and DHA in the form of fish oil. In addition, test your dog's omega-3 levels once or twice yearly to ensure sufficient supplementation. When it comes to ALA, there is frequently a good amount in food, so while it is still excellent to supplement, it is not an absolute necessity.

Vitamin D is another great long-term supplement if your dog is deficient. Many, but not all, dogs I test are low in vitamin D. The amount of vitamin D found in an appropriate multivitamin for animals is fine for all dogs, although it may not be enough. Vitamin D testing is a great way both to quantify the need for supplementation and to confirm that the amount you are supplementing is appropriate.

Periodic

Pretty much everything else on the list can be used on a periodic-rotation basis—and you don't need to use everything. In my experience, most pet owners have a maximum number of supplements they can give before it starts becoming a pain in the you-know-what. I certainly do have clients who are giving their dogs 20 supplements daily, but I'm not expecting you to do this unless you want to.

From a strategic perspective, pick two or three off the list that have complementary actions against the hallmarks of aging. In other words, try to check as many of the nine original boxes as you can with those two or three supplements. Alternatively, there are combination supplements out there that have several of the listed nutrients, so you may be able to check a lot of boxes with just one product.

Either way, give your chosen supplements for a period of time, such as every three months, and then shift to different ones. By adjusting supplements four times per year, you will provide your dog with a wide range of benefits, and it won't become overwhelming.

* * *

There are other longevity-promoting treatments that fall outside the supplement category, such as peptides, pharmaceuticals, and interventional therapies that can be integrated into your dog's longevity plan. We will discuss these in the next chapter. The ultimate goal is to compile everything into a sustainable, comprehensive strategy.

Supplements and the Hallmarks of Aging

	Genomic Instability	Telomere Attrition	Epigenetic Alterations	Loss of Proteostasis
Ashwagandha				
Berberine				
Carotenoids				
CoQ10				
Curcumin				
EGCG				
Essential Fatty Acids				
Fisetin				
Magnesium				
Melatonin				
Mushrooms				
N-Acetylcysteine				
NMN				
Oleuropein Aglycone				
Plasmalogens				
Probiotics				
Pterostilbene				
Pycnogenol				
Quercetin				
Resveratrol				
Selenium				
Serine				
Spermidine				
Suforaphane				
Vitamin A				
Vitamin B				
Vitamin C				
Vitamin D				
Vitamin E				
Vitamin K				
Zinc				

Deregulated Nutrient Sensing	Mitochondrial Dysfunction	Cellular Senescence	Stem Cell Exhaustion	Altered Intercellular Communication

PART IV

THE FUTURE IS HERE

CHAPTER 7

REGENERATIVE THERAPIES AND MEDICINE

The hallmarks of aging provide us with a framework within which we can discover and utilize tools to slow, and possibly even stop, what most people consider inevitable. Understanding the mechanics of what causes our dogs to age and how we can intervene in these processes through nutrition, lifestyle, and supplementation charts a course toward health and longevity for our dogs. But that is only the beginning . . .

We are in a unique position at this moment in time. We are the first generation who has the ability to truly understand and begin to slow the aging process, and the science of longevity is rapidly expanding. New drug therapies are being utilized to slow aging, and some older ones are being repurposed to do the same. Technology is also being leveraged to decelerate the aging process, and treatments for difficult chronic conditions are within our grasp. In this context, longevity medicine is about more than merely addressing the hallmarks of aging—it is about treating medical conditions that will affect both quality and quantity of life.

In this chapter, we will explore longevity therapies and medications that are currently available in the veterinary space and those that will be a part of it in the very near future. As we examine these more advanced longevity options for dogs, it is important to highlight that there is essentially no canine-specific clinical research on these methods. As it turns out, all the therapies mentioned are used on humans with little clinical research as well. Unlike last chapter's discussion of supplements, everything to follow should be done under a veterinarian's supervision. As you are about to see, things are getting very exciting!

OXYGEN THERAPIES

We all know oxygen is important. When we breathe in, oxygen flows into our body, and when we breathe out, carbon dioxide flows out, in the process called respiration. But do you know what happens from there? There is another, much deeper form of respiration called *cellular respiration.*

Earlier, we discussed mitochondrial dysfunction as a hallmark of aging. Mitochondria are the structures within cells that generate the energy that allows every cell in the body to conduct its business. Cellular respiration is a chemical process within mitochondria that generates energy in the form of a molecule called adenosine triphosphate (ATP), and oxygen is required. Without it, the mitochondria's ability to generate ATP is severely limited, and if cells are starved of oxygen long enough, the lack of ATP will cause them to die—or worse.

Decreased oxygenation of tissues is known as *hypoxia.* Hypoxia occurs when the body is not able to deliver oxygen to an area. Systemically, this can be caused by an inability to absorb or circulate oxygen as a result of heart, lung, or circulation disease, as well as anemia (not enough red blood cells). On a more local level, hypoxia occurs after an interruption of circulation due to injury, swelling or inflammation, or occlusion of a blood vessel (embolus). Regardless of the cause, a lack of oxygen dramatically slows tissue healing and regeneration and is associated with cellular aging and potentially the development of cancer.[1, 2, 3]

If a lack of oxygen causes all this trouble, why not just let our dogs breathe oxygen and help them feel and be better? Unfortunately, it's not quite that easy. You see, the red blood cells that carry oxygen are generally 95 percent saturated with oxygen when your dog is breathing regular room air. You can bump that up to 100 percent by having them breathe pure oxygen, but that extra 5 percent really isn't making that much difference. And if the hypoxia is localized in an area with compromised circulation, the body's red blood cells are not able to deliver the oxygen. There are, however, methods to dramatically increase oxygen levels.

Hyperbaric Oxygen Therapy

Hyperbaric oxygen therapy (HBOT) is a procedure in which a patient is placed in a chamber that pressurizes while they—in this case, your dog—breathe 100 percent oxygen. The technology itself goes back as far as the 1600s and was used for a variety of medical issues, albeit with little scientific basis.[4] In more modern times, HBOT was used starting in the 1940s for decompression sickness in deep-sea divers, and later for carbon monoxide poisoning. Since it is unlikely your dog is scuba diving, and carbon monoxide poisoning these days is quite rare even in people, we want to focus on the newer applications of HBOT.

HBOT works through the presence of high concentrations of oxygen and a pressure gradient. Effectively what is happening is that breathing oxygen at high pressure forces it into the bloodstream. The reason HBOT works is because oxygen under pressure dissolves into the plasma (the liquid portion of blood), resulting in the blood being able to carry up to 20 times more oxygen than if the patient were breathing room air alone. As oxygen-saturated blood flows through the body, the oxygen will naturally diffuse into areas where concentrations are lower. Because the oxygen is dissolved in the plasma, it doesn't require a red blood cell to carry it to the site where it is needed. This means that in areas where circulation is compromised due to injury, swelling, and so forth, oxygen can passively diffuse into hypoxic tissues, just like a sponge absorbs water without any assistance. The presence of more oxygen fuels mitochondria, which then generates ATP and allows cells to function and tissues to heal. There is a lot of physics behind the scenes making this all happen, but you get the picture.

In human medicine, HBOT is commonly used in the treatment of nonhealing wounds, such as diabetic ulcers, burns caused by radiation therapy, and deep-seated infections such as osteomyelitis (bone infection).[5, 6] It also has therapeutic effects on certain types of cancers.[7] While we don't see diabetic ulcers in dogs, we certainly do encounter nonhealing wounds of other kinds, as well as radiation burns and difficult-to-treat infections. There are many other therapeutic uses for HBOT in dogs, including organ disease such as pancreatitis or hepatitis, spinal cord compression from a ruptured disc or other trauma, head injury and stroke, and so on. On more than one occasion, I have had a veterinarian refer a patient with an injury or infection that literally threatens both life and limb. We have saved patients from amputations and unquestionably saved lives with HBOT when allopathic medical options have failed.

The effects of regenerative medicine can be subtle, particularly when treating a patient that is largely healthy. There are times, however, when the results for an animal with a severe medical issue are nothing short of miraculous. I've seen more than my share of these "miracles" in my office, and one that always comes to mind is a black Lab named Jackson.

Jackson was an adorable bouncy Labrador with a serious problem. He had developed a swelling on his left hind leg that started as a sore bump near his knee and, within days, progressed to swelling of the entire leg. The swelling had become so bad that the surgeon taking care of Jackson was considering amputation out of concern that it would continue to progress to a point where it would threaten his life. The surgeon, not wanting to amputate if he could avoid it, referred Jackson to my office for treatment.

We immediately began hyperbaric oxygen therapy, and with each treatment there was measurable improvement in the swelling. We were literally measuring the circumference of his swollen leg, and it would decrease by a centimeter or two each treatment. Over the course of a week, the swelling improved to the point where his circulation was no longer compromised, and it was clear surgery would not be necessary. Over a seven-day period, Jackson and his owners went from him needing an amputation to save his life to not needing surgery at all. Everyone from Jackson to his owners to me to his surgeon was thrilled with this amazing turn of events!

You are probably wondering what was wrong with Jackson. Well, during the hyperbaric oxygen treatment, one of his owners went into her yard to a place where Jackson had a habit of lying in the sun. She turned over a small log and found a nest of black widow spiders. It's amazing how much damage such a tiny critter can inflict with one bite. Since then, we have treated more than one suspected spider bite with similar results.

Many people have a concern that using HBOT for the treatment of cancer may "feed" oxygen to cancer cells and make them grow faster. After all, oxygen is a key factor in the production of ATP. Fortunately, this turns out not to be the case. Cancer cells tend to have alterations in their mitochondria that change the way they produce ATP, and in short, they prefer a low-oxygen environment with limited blood supply. Within this hypoxic environment, cancer cells are able to generate energy while shielding themselves from the immune system and anticancer therapeutics such as chemotherapy, herbal therapy, and so forth. Hyperbaric oxygen increases tissue oxygenation throughout the entire body, including tumors. The increase in oxygen concentration within and around cancer can induce apoptosis (programmed cell death) and slow the proliferation of the cancer cells.[8, 9]

HBOT also has specific effects on the hallmarks of aging, including increasing telomere length, decreasing senescent cell burden,[10] and increasing stem cell proliferation, which leads to an increase in the ability of the body to heal wounds and other areas of inflammation and tissue damage.[11] Genomic instability, yet another hallmark, ultimately leads to changes in gene expression and the transcriptome, or the spectrum and function of proteins created from the DNA template. In humans, HBOT has been proven to alter the transcriptome of elderly patients to a younger state.[12] Lastly, HBOT improves cognitive function in older adults, which may be beneficial for dogs, as we do see cognitive decline in some as they age.[13]

One final note regarding HBOT: Therapy requires multiple treatments. Depending on the condition, HBOT therapy for a person might include anywhere from 10 to 50 treatments or more. In veterinary medicine, we aren't always able to do this many treatments, as it would require a significant investment of time and finances on the part of the owner. That said, even fewer treatments than might be conducted in a human with a similar condition can still be effective. HBOT does not enjoy widespread use in veterinary (or human) medicine, although an increasing number of holistic and integrative veterinarians are bringing this technology into their offices. Depending on the indication, HBOT is also covered by some pet insurance policies.

OZONE

You may be familiar with ozone, although probably not in the context of health and longevity. Strictly speaking, ozone is a different molecular form of oxygen. Normally, two oxygen atoms bind together to form a stable molecule known as O_2. This is the form of oxygen you are breathing in the air right now. Ozone is an unstable grouping of three oxygen atoms, or O_3. Environmentally, ozone naturally occurs in the upper atmosphere (the ozone layer) as a result of O_2 being exposed to ultraviolet (UV) light, which converts it to O_3. The ozone layer protects us from many of the harmful effects of UV radiation from the sun. Down here on the surface, ozone is an air pollutant that can cause respiratory irritation.

Given that being directly exposed to ozone gas leads to respiratory irritation, you might ask how ozone can promote health and longevity. Ozone can be administered in multiple ways that do not involve breathing it in. Ozone gas can be given rectally to be absorbed into the bloodstream, subcutaneously (under the skin), or intravenously in the form of ozonated saline that is sometimes mixed with the patient's blood. Ozone gas can also be used topically in a process called limb bagging or through the application of ozonated oil. Lastly, ozone can be used as an oral rinse or consumed in the form of ozonated water.

Ozone works within the body to promote health in more than one way. One of the primary ways is through hormetic stress. This is a process by which an organism experiences a degree of environmental stress that makes the body stronger. Let's say you go to the gym and lift weights and are sore the next day. If your sore muscle were biopsied, what we would see is widespread damage to muscle fibers on a microscopic level. This microtrauma (stress) ultimately stimulates the body to create more and stronger muscle. Hormetic stress to the immune system works very similarly.

I mentioned that the ozone molecule is unstable; it wants to go back to being O_2. The chemical process of ozone breaking apart leads to the formation of hydrogen peroxide and many other compounds in the body that cause oxidation.[14, 15, 16, 17, 18] Antioxidants are compounds that protect the body from the oxidative damage that occurs as a result of normal physiological processes as well as external factors. The "micro-oxidation" caused by the ozone stimulates the body to increase production of natural antioxidants and a variety of other compounds involved with immune system function.[19, 20, 21, 22] So, the hormetic stress caused by ozone leads to a better-functioning immune system.

Because ozone increases the amount of oxygen in tissues, it also supports mitochondrial function and the generation of ATP. Ozone is intensely antimicrobial as well—so much so that it is sometimes used to sterilize surgical instruments—and kills bacteria on contact, making it particularly useful for topical applications to treat infected wounds. In addition, ozone is being researched for its effects on preventing neurodegeneration and cognitive decline in older people. As we previously discussed regarding HBOT, cancer cells thrive in a hypoxic environment, and exposing them to ozone has been shown to induce apoptosis (programmed cell death) through a variety of mechanisms. Additionally, ozone can improve the efficacy of chemotherapy and radiation therapy in cancer patients.[23, 24] Increases in tissue oxygenation and antioxidant production, and subsequent reduction in inflammation, are vital components of keeping cells healthy and promoting longevity.

Like HBOT, ozone therapy is not something every veterinary office offers, but veterinarians offering ozone are out there. There are many protocols for the use of ozone, and a veterinarian experienced with ozone therapy will be able to guide you to the ones that will best fit your dog's needs.

REGENERATIVE MEDICINE

A common theme in longevity medicine is finding ways to utilize the body's natural systems to slow the aging process. One of the most direct ways to do this is by taking healing factors from the body—such as cells, proteins, hormones, and so on that the body naturally produces to facilitate healing—and using them to treat injury or damaged tissues. Using cells or other factors that come from a patient's own body as medicine is called *autologous therapy.* This is most commonly conducted through the use of platelet-rich plasma (PRP) and/or stem cell therapy, and in addition to its therapeutic benefits, it has essentially no risk of side effects, since your dog is receiving something that came from their body. There are also regenerative options that utilize cells or other factors from a healthy animal to benefit one with an issue. Let's explore a few of these options.

Platelet-Rich Plasma

Blood is a combination of solids and liquids. The solids—red blood cells, white blood cells, and platelets—are suspended in liquid (plasma). When the red and white cells are removed from the blood, what remains are platelets suspended in plasma, or platelet-rich plasma (PRP). Platelets play a critical role in blood clotting. If your dog is injured, they help stop the bleeding. The platelets don't stop there, however. They also play a large part in wound healing through promoting the formation of new blood vessels and tissue repair. This is the activity we are looking for by using PRP.

PRP is most commonly used to treat injuries and/or arthritis via injection into the affected site. In human athletes, PRP is commonly a part of the therapy for torn tendons and muscles, rotator-cuff (shoulder) injuries, and so forth. Human medicine is also finding more applications for PRP, including cosmetic procedures and improving the success of hair transplants. While we aren't going to be discussing face-lifts and new hair for your dog, this gives you an idea of the widespread potential uses of something that is already in everyone's body.

In veterinary medicine, the most common use of PRP is to improve functionality and pain in dogs with arthritis. That said, it has also been shown to be effective for the treatment of a variety of other conditions, including tendon injuries, cartilage damage, and bone fractures. Just like in humans, we inject the PRP into and around the site of the injury to help stimulate healing. It can also be applied topically to treat burns, wounds, and even corneal (surface of the eye) injuries.[25] PRP is an accepted form of treatment in veterinary medicine, although not too many general practitioners offer it. More commonly, PRP is administered by a veterinary specialist, such as a surgeon. Even so, it's not a complicated procedure in most cases, and pet insurance will often cover it.

From a longevity perspective, PRP's uses are largely related to promoting healing and limiting pain. While there are likely specific effects on one or more of the hallmarks of aging, they haven't been fully evaluated. Setting aside the hallmarks, aging is ultimately a function of the body no longer being able to repair itself. By intervening with a healing therapy such as PRP to improve mobility and function, we are, by definition, promoting longevity.

Stem Cell Therapy

No doubt you have heard of stem cell therapy. It has been in the news for years both for its potential as an effective therapy and also due to some controversy regarding where the stem cells are harvested. Within the context of veterinary medicine and autologous therapy, all the stem cells we are talking about come from your own dog.

Stem cells are one of the most powerful cell types in the body. Almost all cells in the body have a specific job to do. Heart cells make up the heart muscle, kidney cells make up the kidneys, skin cells make up the skin, and so on. As a rule, these cells will do their job within their particular area of expertise until they are too old to function, and then they are recycled by the body.

When the body needs to replace cells, it has two options. Some cells, such as those within the skin, liver, and GI tract, are able to divide and create new cells to fill the gap. Other tissues, like the heart and kidneys, are not as adept at doing this. When local tissue regeneration is not possible due to either the cell type or extent of damage, stem cells come into play.

Think of stem cells like a young child with her whole life ahead of her. In that moment, she has the potential to become anything. As she gets older and makes choices in her life, the possibilities narrow. At some point (hopefully), she will decide what she wants to do; focus her abilities on that; and emerge as a doctor, lawyer, musician, artist, or anything else. Stem cells are created as a blank slate to provide the body with a source of material to repair and replace tissues throughout the body. To be clear, there are many types of stem cells, and their abilities differ. For the purposes of this discussion, we are focusing on mesenchymal stem cells (MSCs), as these are the ones currently in use in veterinary medicine.

The term *mesenchymal* refers to connective tissue within the body. Connective tissue makes up a broad swath of body structures, including bone, cartilage, blood-vessel walls, fat, and so forth. MSCs are stem cells that can transform into any of these tissues. To use the previous analogy, our little girl has decided she likes science and is focusing her efforts on this. She could become a doctor, a pharmacist, a researcher, or even an astronaut, but most likely law school or a career as a professional musician is off the table. MSCs have a lot of options, but they do not have the ability to transform into non-mesenchymal tissues such as heart cells or brain cells.

In practical terms, MSCs are mostly used for orthopedic conditions, such as arthritis and tendon injuries. The process begins with harvesting the stem cells, which can be achieved from bone marrow or fat. In veterinary medicine, we mostly collect from fat, as it is more easily accessible. The dog is briefly anesthetized, and your veterinarian makes a small incision over their abdomen to collect fat—even thin dogs will have some fatty tissue around their liver. The collection process is quick, as is recovery. The harvested fat is then processed to extract the stem cells. Usually this is done by overnighting the tissue to a lab. The lab extracts the cells, places them in syringes, and overnights them back. Any extra cells are banked for future use.

The process of administering MSCs is usually via a local injection at the site of the problem. Your veterinarian may, for example, inject your dog's arthritic hip or knee. If your dog has a soft-tissue injury such as a biceps or Achilles tendon tear, they would inject the tendon directly. Usually these injections require sedation, but overall the process is quick and relatively painless. Positive effects can be seen from within days to months, depending on the individual and their condition, and sometimes are dramatic: dogs are suddenly running around and feeling better than they have in a long time. All in all, the entire process from harvest to administration takes about 48 hours and can be repeated as necessary. For repeat injections, surgical collection is not required, as the laboratory can use the banked cells collected the first time.

Sometimes MSCs are injected intravenously for other issues such as kidney disease. This sounds like a great idea to address deeper issues, like failing organs and neurologic conditions, but there is a hitch. When we were discussing hyperbaric oxygen, I mentioned how oxygen is "picked up" by the blood in the lungs and then distributed to the entire body. The concern with MSCs is the other side of the circulatory pathway. After the blood delivers oxygen and nutrients to the body, it returns to the heart, where it is pumped back into the lungs. Blood that enters the lungs passes through smaller and smaller blood vessels, down to the level of microcapillaries—tiny vessels that facilitate the exchange of oxygen and carbon dioxide within the lungs. Microcapillaries are 8 to 10 micrometers (microns) in diameter (a micron is 0.001 millimeter). That's barely enough room for red blood cells to fit through, and the larger white blood cells frequently have to squeeze through by changing their shape. MSCs are about 20 micrometers in diameter.

In short, they don't fit, and they get "hung up" in the microcapillaries in the same way peas stay in a strainer after the water has drained. Research shows that few, if any, MSCs can be found anywhere in the body other than the lungs following intravenous infusion.[26, 27] To be clear, this process is not harmful to the lungs, and there is evidence to suggest using MSCs in this way is an effective way to treat diseases of the lung such as emphysema and pulmonary hypertension, among others. It's just not useful to treat other areas of the body.[28, 29]

Very Small Embryonic-Like Stem Cells

A lot of research is being funneled into stem cell therapy for obvious reasons. The prospect of being able to regenerate damaged or diseased areas of the body is highly appealing. Beyond MSCs, whose advantages and limitations we just discussed, other types of stem cells are under study.

Embryonic stem cells are taken from fetal tissue and have the ability to transform into any cell type in the body. They can also be collected from umbilical-cord blood from newborns. Both have the potential to help aging dogs, but as a practical matter neither of these are viable options given the ethical considerations of collecting fetal tissue from pregnant dogs and the fact that few puppies are born in a hospital setting, making umbilical-cord-blood storage impossible.

Induced pluripotent stem cells have similar properties to embryonic stem cells, but they are created from "regular" cells. Essentially, cells from the body can be treated with specific compounds known as Yamanaka factors and can be transformed backward into a cell very similar to an embryonic stem cell. The researcher who discovered this process, Shinya Yamanaka, received a Nobel Prize in 2012 for this work. There is a lot of potential here, but these stem cells are not ready for prime time, as they appear to be prone to causing benign tumors known as teratomas.

There is another type of stem cell you have likely never heard of. In fact, most veterinarians and physicians have never heard of them. *Very small embryonic-like stem cells* (VSELs) were originally described in the scientific literature as early as 2008, but their function—and in some circles, their very existence—was questioned.[30] These cells are present in tissues throughout the body and circulate through the blood. They appear to be the body's version of reserve embryonic stem cells. In other words, they are able to transform into any tissue type in the body, as opposed to more specialized stem cells like MSCs. As the name would imply, VSELs are small, around 5 micrometers. This, of course, means they can live in circulating blood and pass through the lungs, unlike the much larger MSCs. Although research is ongoing, it is safe to say VSELs are used by the body to repair tissues in the event of injury or other damage.[31]

Another fascinating characteristic of VSELs is that they don't appear to age.[32] Other stem cells tend to be less effective when they are collected from an older patient. (Remember, stem cell exhaustion is one of the hallmarks of aging.) The trouble is, more often than not, the patient who needs stem cell therapy is middle-aged or older. VSELs are essentially dormant until they are needed, and this metabolic inactivity means they don't age like other cells. Thus, the

VSELs of a 15-year-old dog are, at least in theory, as potent as the day the dog was born.

I suspect you are starting to see what is so interesting about VSELs. It appears they have the benefits of embryonic stem cells, do not necessitate collection under difficult or controversial circumstances, and are "good as new," regardless of the age of the patient. Until recently, however, all of this was purely a laboratory exercise and not used in clinical practice as a result of the medical community being slow to realize the potential of these newly discovered cells. Thankfully, that is changing.

A physician and researcher in Southern California named Todd Ovokaitys has discovered some other interesting properties of VSELs and found a way to utilize them to treat patients.[33, 34] Dr. Todd, as he is called, was doing VSEL research and had the cells in a dish. He used a laser to project a beam through the center of the dish for three minutes and something pretty surprising happened. The dormant VSELs began to rapidly reproduce, and instead of being distributed throughout the dish, the cells moved into a line along the axis of where the laser had been. To make a very complex story short, the laser "woke up" the VSELs and changed the expression of proteins on the surface of the cells, making them adhere to one another. The cells effectively became "sticky."

This discovery led Dr. Todd to develop a procedure to extract and separate VSELs from a blood sample in much the same way we discussed earlier for PRP. In fact, this procedure is really a combination of PRP and stem cell therapy. The PRP, which contains VSELs, is exposed to a very specific type of laser (also designed by Dr. Todd) that wakes up the VSELs. At this point, the VSEL/PRP solution can either be administered directly into an affected area, such as an arthritic joint, or be given intravenously, since the

VSELs are so small that they pass through the lungs with no problem.

Once the cells are administered, the same laser that was used to wake up the VSELs is directed at the body part(s) being targeted for the treatment. As the cells move through the circulation and past the area being lasered, they become "sticky" and tend to stay in that area. The goal is for the VSELs to be concentrated in the area of the body being treated. This is of particular value for internal organs or the brain and spinal cord, as these areas are difficult to inject directly.

VSEL therapy holds a lot of promise, and there are reports from humans being treated that are nothing short of miraculous, such as people's heart function improving so much they are no longer in need of a transplant, along with reports of improved vision, joint function, cognition, and so forth. While studies have evaluated the use of VSELs for the treatment of conditions such as heart disease and for the rejuvenation of tissues, there are currently no published clinical trials on the procedure developed by Dr. Todd, although that is likely to change.[35, 36]

On the veterinary side, I am extremely fortunate to be the first veterinarian to use Dr. Todd's procedure on patients, and we are seeing similar results. When we first started offering VSELs in my office, I was looking for patients for whom I felt we could make a big difference. Many of these first patients were dogs with arthritis or neurologic diseases. One of them, however, was a young dog named Beau with a heart condition known as dilated cardiomyopathy. Beau's heart condition was so severe that his cardiologist had given him only a couple of months to live. I remembered Dr. Todd telling me he was seeing successes in people with severe heart disease, so I really wanted to try to see if we could help.

Beau's owner flew him up to Oakland from Los Angeles, and we treated him with VSELs. About six weeks later, he had a recheck with the cardiologist, who was shocked to see Beau's heart function had improved significantly! There was no explanation for this other than the VSEL therapy. Beau ultimately lived well over one year after the single VSEL treatment . . . far longer than anyone expected. Unfortunately, we were not able to treat Beau again for nonmedical-related reasons. Multiple VSEL treatments over time would have likely been enormously beneficial. Even with that said, a single injection of stem cells provided Beau with over one year of quality time, and I am thrilled we were able to give that to him.

While VSEL therapy is not currently a widely available option for veterinary or human patients, it will be found in more and more clinics over time. Most patients do require more than one treatment, and the best results appear to be when the treatment is repeated at regular intervals, somewhere between one to four times yearly.

MICROBIOME RESTORATIVE THERAPY

Microbiome restorative therapy (MBRT) is the more formal name for fecal transplants (I'm guessing you probably just made an unpleasant sound). A fecal transplant is exactly what it sounds like: a stool sample (feces) from a healthy dog is put into a dog that has medical issues, such as chronic gastrointestinal disease, allergies, or other conditions associated with an imbalance of the immune system.

As I mentioned in the discussion of probiotics, 70 percent of the immune system lives in the gut, meaning imbalances of gut flora can have a broad impact on overall health, far beyond signs of GI distress. Imbalances of gut flora have, in fact, been linked to allergies, cognitive dysfunction, and Parkinson's disease in humans.[37, 38, 39] Probiotics can help restore healthy gut flora, but there are limits to what they can do. Probiotics work by creating an environment in the gut that is friendly to beneficial bacteria and does not support the growth of harmful ones. There is a common misconception that probiotics are recolonizing the gut with new bacteria, but this is not the case. Not long after you stop giving them, the bacterial strains in the probiotic are gone. This is why you need to keep giving them long term.

MBRT works differently, because it can help restore healthy gut flora for the long term. Dogs may have unhealthy flora for a variety of reasons, including poor diet, antibiotic use, and chemotherapy.[40, 41] Sometimes probiotics are enough to restore the balance, but in more severe cases, MBRT is required. More specifically pertaining to aging and longevity, fecal transplantations from young mice into older mice have been shown to reverse hallmarks of aging in the gut, eyes, and brain.[42]

In veterinary medicine, fecal transplantation was pioneered by a veterinarian named Margo Roman in Massachusetts, and she has been using MBRT alongside ozone therapy for years, often with dramatically positive results. She also coined the term *microbiome restorative therapy*. Fecal material from prescreened healthy dogs is administered rectally, and sometimes orally, in the form of frozen fecal material in capsules. The procedure frequently is repeated several times over a period of months to achieve the greatest effects.

Other protocols utilize freeze-dried fecal transplant material given orally in capsules, although I have not seen dramatically positive results with this method. This probably goes without saying, *but don't try this at home*. Work with a veterinarian with experience in fecal transplantation.

PLASMA REPLACEMENT

As we have previously discussed, plasma is the liquid fraction of blood. You can also think of it as blood minus the red and white blood cells. Platelets may or may not be present, depending on if we are discussing pure plasma or platelet-rich plasma. Regardless, plasma isn't merely the liquid blood cells are suspended in. It has a significant purpose, including maintaining osmotic pressure, or the balance of fluid inside and outside cells. It also serves as a carrier for vital blood proteins, sugar, fats, and cell-signaling compounds like hormones.

Scientists have been evaluating the effects of taking blood from one animal and putting it into another for well over 100 years. These studies have led to advancements in multiple fields of medicine, including immunology, oncology, and endocrinology. There is also an interesting facet of this type of study pertaining to longevity.

Initial research into this field is a little weird. In a process called heterochronic parabiosis, researchers took an old mouse and a young mouse and literally sewed them together so they shared a circulatory system.[43] Not necessarily the most humane research trial, but most of these things occurred 50 or more years ago. Setting aside the creepy factor, something really interesting came of these studies. When the mice of different ages were surgically connected, the young mouse got "older" and the old mouse got "younger," raising the question of how the components of blood are related to aging.

If old blood promotes "oldness" and young blood promotes "youngness," what factors are at play? If putting young blood into an older animal has a positive effect, is it because there are components in young blood that promote youth, or is it that we are diluting out factors in old blood that promote aging? Conversely, if old blood will age a young animal, are we infusing aging factors into young blood, or are we diluting out the youthful factors and making them less abundant? It would appear the answer is yes across the board. Since no one in their right mind is advocating dogs being surgically connected or using young dogs as blood donors to keep older ones healthy, is there a less vampirish way to leverage this very interesting information? It turns out there are several.

The least complicated solution is therapeutic plasma exchange. You are probably familiar with donating plasma, and perhaps you have even done it. You donate blood, and then the plasma is removed and your red blood cells are returned through an IV infusion. From a longevity perspective, the same process can be done in order to dilute out the "old" factors in blood.[44, 45] It's kind of like doing a half water change in a fish tank. The water becomes much cleaner, even though you didn't replace all of it. The challenge here from a dog-treatment perspective is that there aren't really facilities that will do this. Plasma is extracted at facilities that supply veterinarians with blood-transfusion products, but this is not the kind of equipment any veterinarian has in their office.

Another approach is to add youthful factors to an older dog's body through a plasma transfusion from a younger dog. The issue here, of course, is that using the blood of young animals as a longevity therapeutic for older animals is unethical, pure and simple. There is simply no way to make this okay. That said, there are groups currently working on creating synthetic products that mimic "young plasma." In the future, it may be possible to purchase a bag of synthetic "young dog plasma" and infuse it into older animals in order to promote longevity.

Perhaps the most complicated way to "clean up" an older person's blood is through plasmapheresis. In this process, a patient is hooked up to a machine that extracts blood, cleans the plasma, and then returns it. This process is similar to dialysis for kidney patients. As you might imagine, plasmapheresis is very expensive and, as such, not currently available for veterinary patients.

Plasma replacement shows a lot of promise, but we are still a ways away from this being a practical component of longevity therapy for your dog. It is definitely something to keep an eye out for in the future.

DRUGS

Considering how much science is involved with the quest for longevity, you might think there would be more pharmaceuticals available. Undoubtedly, drugs will be developed specifically for the purposes of longevity medicine, but for now this list is relatively short. That said, the two drugs discussed below are powerful options for our quest to help our dogs live longer and better.

Rapamycin

Rapamycin is a drug with a fascinating history. It was originally discovered as a compound produced by a particular bacteria present on Easter Island. The name, in fact, comes from the traditional one for Easter Island, Rapa Nui. Rapamycin has conventionally been used in organ-transplant patients to help prevent tissue rejection, and in recent years it has received a lot of attention for its longevity-promoting properties.

In Chapter 2, we discussed the mammalian target of rapamycin, or mTOR. This pathway helps regulate nutrient sensing in the body and specifically promotes tissue growth, which can be good or bad, depending on what tissue is growing. Rapamycin inhibits mTOR and thus slows tissue growth. At appropriate doses, rapamycin has anticancer properties; supports cardiovascular, immune system, and cognitive function; and helps animals live longer.[46, 47] In short, rapamycin is one of the most interesting and promising pharmaceutical interventions currently available in the longevity space.

Rapamycin dosing has to be done very carefully, however, and it is not something to be given every day. You may remember we previously discussed the balance between mTOR and AMPK, which modulates the body's ability to both create and break down cells. Both are critical to health and longevity, and everything has to be in balance. Many longevity-focused physicians recommend cycling rapamycin use in humans once weekly, and an ongoing research trial known as the Dog Longevity Project is evaluating the effects of rapamycin on dogs.[48] I am intentionally not providing dosing information on rapamycin, because this drug can be dangerous if used improperly. Please only try this under direct veterinary supervision.

Dasatinib

Dasatinib is a chemotherapy drug used to treat leukemia in people. Pharmacologically speaking, it is known as a tyrosine kinase inhibitor. Tyrosine kinase is a protein that signals cells to divide, and in some cancer cells, the protein is abnormal and leads to uncontrolled cellular division. Dasatinib blocks the action of tyrosine kinase and thus can slow the progression of cancers like leukemia in humans.

Dasatinib, in conjunction with quercetin (see Chapter 6), is also a potent senolytic, meaning it has the ability to kill senescent cells in the body. As you recall, senescent cells no longer function as healthy cells, and they also resist being eliminated by the body. Cellular senescence is one of the hallmarks of aging, because these cells frequently secrete chemical compounds that promote the formation of more senescent cells, which decreases the body's ability to function optimally (aging) and, in the process, potentially promotes the formation of cancer.[49, 50] Senolytics have also been demonstrated to increase physical function and improve life span in research animals through a variety of cellular pathways. The combination of dasatinib and quercetin has shown impressive senolytic effect and is one of the more promising approaches to address this particular hallmark of aging.[51, 52, 53] To my knowledge, dasatinib has not been used in dogs for longevity purposes . . . yet.

Senolytic cells take time to accumulate, which means senolytics can be used intermittently in a "hit and run" approach.[54] The goal is to reduce your dog's senescent cell burden and then stop the treatment. Potent senolytics like dasatinib are not, and should not be, given on a regular basis. Remember, this is not a supplement with a wide range of safety. Dasatinib can cause side effects, such as heart and lung damage, if used long term or at improper doses. In addition, it's important to note that dasatinib has been studied in dogs as a chemotherapy agent but not as a senolytic. There is every reason to presume combining it with quercetin could be an effective antiaging therapy for dogs, but more research is required for us to know for sure.

PEPTIDE THERAPY

Amino acids are strung together based on instructions from DNA to form peptides, polypeptides, and ultimately proteins. Peptides and polypeptides are utilized by the body for a variety of reasons, including functioning as hormones, growth factors, neurotransmitters, and other cell-signaling compounds that provide instructions to the body.

Peptide therapy is the use of peptides either orally or via injection to promote certain processes in the body that help treat medical conditions and promote longevity. They are frequently "stacked," meaning a patient will receive more than one peptide in a given treatment cycle. Treatment cycles usually are around two months, although this can vary depending on the individual and goals of therapy. There is a long list of peptides being used for this purpose. Currently, peptide therapy is not being widely offered in the veterinary space, although this is likely to change, so it is important for you, as a longevity-focused dog parent, to be aware of it. The following are a few of the most commonly used peptides in humans that are also promising for dogs.

BPC 157

Body protection compound 157 (BPC 157) is a peptide that is naturally produced in the stomach.[55, 56, 57] Its purpose is to accelerate healing-and-repair processes in the gastrointestinal tract. Used therapeutically, BPC 157 has been shown to promote the healing of the GI tract, as well as most other tissues, including muscles, ligaments, tendons, bone, organs such as the brain, the spinal cord, and so forth. It has also been shown to promote wound healing and is being investigated as a therapy for various central nervous system disorders through its effect on the gut-brain axis. While all these applications will likely be beneficial in dogs, the most promising immediate use would be for chronic gastrointestinal conditions, such as inflammatory bowel disease, as well as for the soreness, aches, and pains associated with injury and aging. BPC 157 can be administered orally for GI-related issues or as an injection for musculoskeletal or other concerns.

Thymosin Beta 4

Thymosin beta 4 is a peptide produced by all tissues and cells in the body. Similar to BPC 157, thymosin beta 4 has tissue-regeneration properties and has been shown to have regenerative effects in the heart, liver, and eye and in wound healing. Because of its ability to mobilize stem cells in the body, it is also being evaluated as a primary therapy for longevity.[58, 59, 60, 61, 62]

There is a degree of controversy surrounding thymosin beta 4. It has been suggested that some cancer cells overexpress thymosin beta 4, raising concerns that administering it could promote cancer. The research evidence here is not strong, and there is also research to suggest the opposite, but nonetheless it is concerning for some people.[63, 64, 65] In response to these concerns, fragments of thymosin beta 4 can be used rather than the entire peptide. The full compound consists of 43 amino acids. It has been found that the fragment containing amino acids 1–4 is anti-inflammatory and the one containing 17–23 promotes tissue healing. There is no evidence to connect the fragments to cancer. Thymosin beta 4, or fragments thereof, is administered via injection, most commonly for immune system support, to decrease inflammation, and for tissue generation and the promotion of longevity.

CJC 1295 + Ipamorelin

The story of CJC 1295 and ipamorelin is really the story of growth hormone (GH). GH is produced in the pituitary gland at the base of the brain, and as the name would suggest, it plays a large role in growth and development.[66, 67, 68] It stimulates bone and muscle growth, regulating body fat levels, and even brain development and function. As our dogs get older, levels of GH naturally decline. This is one of the major reasons why muscle mass decreases and body fat tends to increase with advancing age.

In the human longevity space, there are treatment protocols where people receive human growth hormone (HGH). There is, however, some concern that long-term use of HGH could lead to problems such as the onset of diabetes or cancer. Most longevity doctors prefer to encourage the body to produce its own GH through the use of peptides, rather than giving GH directly. CJC 1295 and ipamorelin are used, almost always in combination, to stimulate production of GH from the pituitary gland. Indications for use include building muscle, decreasing body fat, and facilitating healing of injuries, as well as increasing sleep quality and cognitive function. CJC 1295 and ipamorelin are administered via injection.

* * *

As you can see, there are quite a few regenerative treatments available for dogs and even more in the "coming soon" category. These technological advances are going to have a large impact on the health and longevity of our current—and future—pets, and with more and more longevity-focused options becoming available, one of the facets of animal health that will turn out to be increasingly important will be our ability to monitor health in real time. This emerging technology will become indispensable to supporting animal health, and it is the topic of the upcoming chapter.

CHAPTER 8

TRACKING HEALTH

If you have read all the chapters to this point, you know more about longevity medicine than most veterinarians and physicians. This is cutting-edge information much of the medical community has yet to embrace. The final piece of the longevity puzzle is addressing the single greatest challenge of veterinary medicine and animal health in general: How do you know when your pet is sick?

In this chapter I'll alert you to some of the warning signs of a sick dog and teach you how to be more mindful of subtle changes. I'll also introduce some potential new technologies that could really help when it comes to early detection of health issues.

OUR LYING BEST FRIENDS

As nonverbal patients, animals can't tell us when something is wrong. But the challenge we face goes even deeper. Not only can they not communicate to us verbally when something is wrong, but they flat-out won't communicate this at all. Our dogs are 100 percent honest with this one exception, and the reason is simple: an animal in the wild that looks sick or injured becomes a target for predators.

Despite tens of thousands of years of domestication, our dogs are still hardwired to make it look like everything is okay, even when it isn't.

The practical result of our dogs lying to us about not feeling well is that by the time they look sick, they probably have been sick for a while. This leads to delays in seeking medical care and late-stage diagnoses. You don't need to have an advanced degree in medicine to understand that making a diagnosis when a disease is in an advanced stage leads to fewer treatment options and, sadly, poorer outcomes.

This inability to diagnose problems early has plagued dog owners and veterinarians since there have been dog owners and veterinarians. Chances are pretty good you have had a personal experience with a dog where a problem was diagnosed much later than you would have preferred. As a veterinarian, I deal with this every day. People frequently will say, "He was fine last week." The truth is, he wasn't, but he wanted you to think he was.

It would be easy to say the answer here is that as dog parents, we all need to be more observant. There is some truth to this statement, and certainly one of the key early indicators of a problem in a dog is a change in their routine. You see, dogs like routine. They eat at the same time every day, they wake up and go to sleep with consistency, and their walk schedule is generally regular as well. When you see your dog changing their routine without an obvious reason, it is a signal for you to pay close attention. Changes might be subtle, such as eating slower or not wanting breakfast until a little later than normal. They may be drinking more water than usual or sleeping more or sleeping in different places than they typically do. Perhaps they aren't as enthused to go out on a walk or aren't as interested in playtime. *Any change in their routine can be an early indicator of a medical problem.* When in doubt, contact your veterinarian.

If your gut tells you there is something wrong, be persistent and get your dog seen and evaluated.

Being more attentive and recognizing subtle changes in behavior is an important step toward earlier diagnosis. That said, sometimes the changes may be too subtle to notice, they may occur when you are not in the house, or none may be present at all. We need to find a better, more reliable way to get clued in to medical problems as early as possible. Finding the solution to the nonverbal, symptom-hiding dog is not simple, but it is attainable. In essence, we have to figure out how to "listen" in ways we never have before.

A NEW WAY TO LISTEN

You have undoubtedly heard of wearable devices for people, such as Fitbit, Apple Watch, WHOOP, or Oura Ring, among others. These devices monitor biometric parameters, such as heart rate, heart rhythm, and pulse oximetry. This data is then utilized to provide insight into the wearer's health. If you have a wearable device, you are seeing things like "sleep scores," "recovery scores," heart rate variability, calories burned, and a host of other metrics that the device uses to monitor your health and well-being. It will give you insight into how effective your exercise is and even how much you should exercise on a given day based on how well you slept the night before. Having this window into how your body is working is pretty cool.

Allow me to recount a quick personal story: I have a wearable that I enjoy using for all of the above reasons. A while back, I woke up one morning and received an alert from the device's app on my phone that I had never seen before: my respiration rate overnight was higher than my average, and this is frequently a sign of a person getting sick. I felt fine that morning, but the next day I was COVID-positive.

So, my wearable effectively knew I had COVID the day before I began to feel sick. In other words, it didn't need anything from me in order to detect a problem. Consider this technology from an animal-health perspective. Let's say a dog owner receives a message on their phone saying that their dog's average heart rate and respiration rate have increased by 10 percent over the past day or two, and their activity level is down a little. Now, a 10 percent change in respiration is too subtle for even the most diligent dog owner to recognize, but these changes are almost certainly a sign of a problem. It could be the dog is in pain or has heart disease or any number of other things, and determining the specifics is where your veterinarian comes in. Being alerted to minute changes like these could avert a scenario where days, weeks, or even months later, there is a "hair on fire" trip to the emergency room that may not have a good ending. Being able to intervene before issues escalate is the key to more successful treatment outcomes.

Here is another real-world story (this one about a cat): A while ago I received a text from a friend with a video clip of his cat. He said she was not acting right and wanted to know what I thought. I looked at the video, and she was clearly in respiratory distress. Given that my friend and his cat are in Southern California and I am up in NorCal, it wasn't anything I could personally attend to. I directed him to take his cat to the emergency clinic immediately, where she was diagnosed with congestive heart failure. Thankfully, she was treated and survived, but things could have easily gone the other way. If my friend had been alerted when his cat's respiration rate first began to elevate, his cat could have been diagnosed and treated before things became life-threatening.

ADVANTAGES OF BIOMETRIC MONITORING

In the near future, biometric monitoring in the form of wearables for dogs on a collar or harness will become standard of care for people who want to be proactive with their dogs' health. Coupled with the wearable, imagine an app that can tell you if your dog is getting the optimal amount of exercise, give you guidance on how much food they should be eating based on their health and activity level, and provide advice on medical concerns. Plus, all of this data would be sent to your veterinarian as well so they have the same window into your dog that you do. The entire point of this book is for you to learn how to intervene early when it comes to your dog's life span and health span. Wearables like these will, for the first time, put us in the driver's seat and allow us to get ahead of health problems before they become symptomatic.

By now, you are starting to see the diagnostic value in a device that can provide you with information about subtle changes in your dog's vital signs, and the applications don't stop there. The same device will be incredibly useful in monitoring treatment. Imagine your dog has arthritis and your veterinarian is providing treatment. If your dog's wearable shows their heart rate and respiration rate are down and activity level is up, that is a pretty good indication treatment is working. Conversely, if no changes are seen, then you know you have to try something else. A wearable could be used in exactly the same way to monitor efficacy of all the longevity-focused interventions we have discussed thus far.

Biometric wearables will actually become more effective the longer they are used, because the software and artificial intelligence (AI) will learn your dog's patterns and be even better able to predict problems with the slightest indication of change. This kind of data will, of course, be valuable for your individual dog, but it will also benefit the entire population of dogs using wearables. The aggregate of tens or hundreds of thousands of dogs providing input will help the AI learn more and faster, and eventually there will be known biometric patterns for specific diseases, breeds, ages, and so forth. The applications of this kind of data in both the patient-care and research arenas are staggering. Biometric wearable technology has the power to dramatically change animal health care, lower costs for pet owners, and promote longevity in our furry family members.

WHAT'S COMING NEXT?

You may be aware of some wearables for dogs currently on the market such as Whistle and Fi. Most of these don't, however, monitor actual vital signs, and the few that do have limitations that make them impractical for daily home use. A typical device only measures movement through the use of an accelerometer and a GPS tracker. This is helpful in knowing how active your dog has been, and it can even be used to alert you if your dog has been scratching a lot and potentially if they have a seizure. In other words, these devices will give you some insight into your dog's health, but without vital-signs data, there is only so much these products can tell you.

Things would be easy if we could just take the technology used for wearables for people and apply it to dogs. I'm sure you have already deduced the problem here—fur. Wearables for people collect data by being in direct contact with the skin. This allows a variety of sensors to detect what is happening in the wearer's body. If you take your Apple Watch and place it on the top of your head, it won't work, because it can't read through your hair (assuming, of course, that you have hair).

So the key to a world-changing wearable for dogs begins with noncontact vital-sign sensing. There are some technologies out there that are approaching these capabilities, and it is only a matter of time before you can go online and purchase such a device. If we look even a little further down the road, the evolution beyond wearables will be implantable technology. I'm sure you are familiar with microchips for dogs. These chips, about the size of a grain of rice, encode a unique ID number that can be used to reunite a lost pet with their owner. A veterinarian or animal-services department simply waves a scanner over the dog and it provides the number, which is stored in a national database. When the chips are implanted, the owner registers their information with the chip number, so when we call with a chip number, they can tell us how to contact the owner. Contrary to what a lot of people seem to think, microchips cannot be used to track your dog. They can only be "read" by a scanner that is inches away from the microchip. Big Brother is definitely not watching you or your dog via their chip.

One interesting upgrade to microchips recently is that they can also tell your dog's body temperature. Pretty cool, right? As technology advances, it is likely these chips will have onboard sensors that can detect a range of biometrics, from heart rate to blood parameters like oxygenation and blood sugar, kidney function, and so forth. When this happens, it will be a sea change for the world of health care for both humans and animals. Talk about early diagnosis!

Whether the monitor is wearable or implantable, the purpose of the sensor is really only to feed information to the artificial-intelligence systems that will perform the real magic. Artificial intelligence, machine learning, and neural nets are already changing the world, as computer systems are now able to "learn." Just like we humans learn through our experiences, computer systems learn through data input. The more data you feed them, the more they learn. In the case of wearables for dogs, the more dogs there are wearing devices and the longer they wear them, the speedier the learning and the better the predictive accuracy of the software. When we reach the point where hundreds of thousands of dogs have wearables, the amount of data collected will be enormous, and subsequently the power of the predictive algorithms will be immense! Wearable biometric monitors are in the "coming soon" category, and implantables are "coming later," but definitely keep an eye out. It won't be too long before wearables for both humans and animals will become as ubiquitous as cell phones, and dedicated pet owners wouldn't dream of having a dog without one.

How Can I Track My Dog's Health Right Now?

Our tools for health tracking for dogs now rely on an observant owner and a veterinarian's ability to run diagnostic tests such as blood work, X-rays, and so on. Owners can also weigh their dog on a regular schedule at home. All of these are great options, but they don't hold a candle to real-time vital-sign and activity monitoring when it comes to promoting health and longevity.

* * *

Wearable health monitors for dogs will be the next evolution of their health care. When we combine this with all the other facets of care we have discussed that promote longevity, you can begin to see how we are going to be able to make a huge impact on both quality and quantity of life. The only thing left for us to do now is to take all this information and turn it into something actionable for you, as a pet parent.

CHAPTER 9

OVERVIEW AND SUMMARY OF RECOMMENDATIONS

By now, you have a familiarity with the hallmarks of aging and how various interventions can impact them and, ultimately, prolong your dog's life span and health span. The key to successfully implementing a longevity plan for your furry family members is creating one that will be effective and sustainable *for you*. If the plan is too complicated or expensive to adhere to, chances are that you won't keep up with it in the long term, so keep this in mind as you decide how to proceed.

What follows is a brief review of information from the previous chapters, which will help lay the groundwork by suggesting what to prioritize and ways to implement a longevity strategy for your dog. The prerequisite to success at anything is building a strong foundation. Using the pyramid of longevity as a model, let's break down what actions are recommended at each level. The lower the level, the more important and impactful your actions will be with respect to promoting longevity for your dog.

Remember, none of this is written in stone; feel free to make adjustments according to what works best for you and your dog. The point here is to implement strategies that are sustainable with regard to your time and resources. Even if diet and lifestyle are as much as you can take on, optimizing those will have an enormous impact on your dog's life.

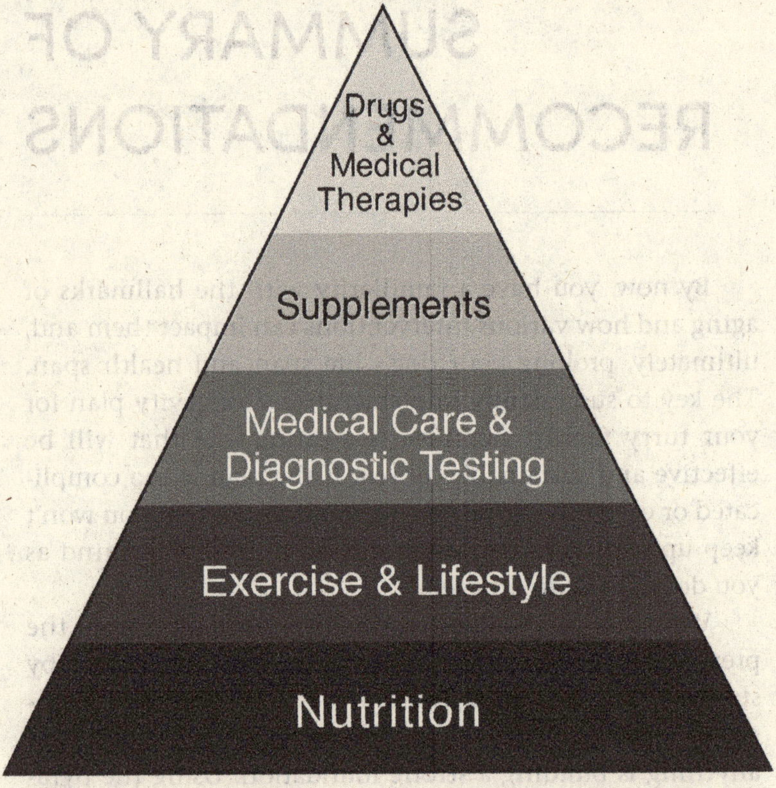

LEVEL 1: NUTRITION

It all starts here. Nutrition is the foundation of good health, full stop. Don't spend a minute or a dime on anything before you have optimized your dog's nutrition as much as you can. Think of nutrition and lifestyle as the tree upon which all the ornaments (diagnostics, supplements, drugs, and procedures) are hung. Strengthen the tree before you do anything else.

In principle, optimizing nutrition for your dog is easy. It is easier, in fact, than optimizing your own. You are in complete control of what your dog eats, and as such, you can make sure every bite of food they take is optimized. The goal is to get as close to a balanced, fresh, whole-food diet as possible.

Here is what you need to know:

- Foods can be commercially prepared in cooked, raw, or freeze-dried form, or they can be homemade from a balanced recipe.
- Balanced diets are important. At least 80 percent of your dog's food intake should be a balanced diet of nutritionally sound, healthy food that does not include treats or scraps from the table.
- Rotate through different recipes over time to provide your dog with a spectrum of nutrients.
- Frequency of diet rotation depends on how easily your dog can adapt to the change. Once they are accustomed to a variety of foods, most don't require a transition from one to the next, but if your dog has a sensitive GI tract, consider doing a gradual transition from one recipe to another three to four times annually.
- Fresh-food diets are more expensive than kibble or canned. If you are unable to feed 100 percent balanced fresh foods, supplement fresh food on top of high-quality canned food or kibble.

- Do not overfeed—aim for a body condition score of 5 on a scale of 9 (see chart on page 77).
- If possible, feed once daily.

LEVEL 2: EXERCISE AND LIFESTYLE

Along with good nutrition, the benefits of exercise and lifestyle are intuitively obvious, although when it comes to dogs, you do need to determine what is best for each as an individual based on their breed, temperament, and other factors. Keep in mind, exercise is about both physical and mental health. High-energy dogs in particular need to work off some energy so they can be calm and relaxed at home. In addition, the *type* of exercise your dog gets is as important as the time spent exercising. Minimize high-impact activities, in favor of low-impact ones like walking, hiking, swimming, and playing at the dog park. Remember, dogs live in the moment, which means they aren't generally considering the consequences of their actions. As such, we have to be their conscience when it comes to enforcing rest and water breaks. Don't let your dog overexert themselves.

The other side of the coin here is lifestyle. Stress and anxiety of any kind are detrimental to good health. Clearly, life has its stressful moments for both dogs and humans. This is more about your dog's day-to-day life, which should focus on them feeling safe and secure. A dog also feeds off their owner's emotional state. If you are a high-stress individual or live in a high-stress environment, both your dog's health and your own are likely being impacted. For both of your sakes, consider what it will take to turn down the heat and find ways for each of you to decompress. The foundation of a good lifestyle for dogs is one that's compatible with yours. High-energy dogs are likely going to do better with owners who can spend a lot of time outdoors, while smaller "couch dogs" may prefer to share more quiet time at home.

Here are your guidelines:

- Regular, daily exercise is important for both you and your dog.
- The amount and type of exercise that are best vary based on age, breed, physical conditioning, and so forth.
- Overexercising or a lot of high-impact activity (Frisbee catching, ball chasing, and so on) can have significant long-term effects that can decrease health span and life span.
- Understanding your dog's natural energy levels and personality will improve both their quality of life and yours.
- Having a stable home where your dog feels safe and secure promotes happiness and longevity.
- Dogs enjoy consistency and routine.
- Dogs are social creatures; they like to interact with other dogs and people.

LEVEL 3: MEDICAL CARE AND DIAGNOSTIC TESTING

With regard to specific medical care, the biggest take-home here is that your job is to be an advocate for your dog, especially if you don't have access to a holistic or integrative veterinarian. This means asking questions (respectfully) when your veterinarian makes recommendations for vaccines, medications, surgeries, and so forth. For example, just because your dog is "due" for something doesn't necessarily mean it has to, or even should, happen, and not every infection requires oral antibiotics. Remember, ideal medical care is personalized to the individual animal, and no one protocol is appropriate for all dogs. This is true for all facets of veterinary care.

As your dog's advocate, be on the lookout for changes in behavior. If your dog breaks their daily routine and there isn't a clear explanation why, you need to pay close attention. This is frequently the first sign of medical problems. The key to success with veterinary care is to be proactive. Don't wait until your dog is sick to get them looked at. An ounce of prevention really is worth a pound of cure.

For even greater insight into how your dog is doing, biometric wearables are the next big thing. Many of the current products can provide you with some data regarding your dog's activity level, but the next-generation devices on the horizon will monitor vital signs and utilize artificial intelligence to predict illness at its earliest stages. These wearables will revolutionize animal health and veterinary medicine in profound ways.

Dental care is critically important to health and longevity, and this is something that really is on you as your dog's caretaker. Yes, your veterinarian can clean your dog's teeth, but that usually necessitates general anesthesia, which is always a risk. Additionally, imagine if you had your teeth cleaned by your dentist and then you didn't brush them until your appointment the following year. That is what happens all the time with dogs, and it leads to problems for middle-aged and older dogs. You want to have a routine at home that includes brushing, all-natural dental chews, and maybe the occasional raw bone to chew on.

The big advantage of diagnostic testing is that it allows us to be more objective about our longevity plan for our dogs. There certainly are facets of our strategy that can, and should, be implemented regardless of test results. There are other facets that we do not yet have the ability to test for. That said, measuring specific parameters that affect aging allows us to implement therapies and subsequently observe their effects. Few things in health care are one-size-fits-all, and an intervention that works for one dog may not work for another. By utilizing diagnostic testing, we can determine how well our treatments are working and, most important, when they are *not* working, so we can try more or different therapeutics.

Some tests—complete blood count and blood chemistries—can easily be run by your veterinarian. Some tests—profiling genetic predispositions for disease (Embark, Wisdom Panel), oxidative stress (CellBIO), and food sensitivity (NutriScan)—can be done at home if your veterinarian doesn't offer them. Other diagnostics—vitamin and mineral levels, omega fatty acid levels, cancer screening, and age profiles such as DNA methylation and telomere testing—require blood samples, yet are frequently not offered by most veterinarians. But with the information provided in Chapter 2, you may be able to convince your veterinarian to help you submit these to the appropriate labs.

One other note about diagnostic testing: There is definitely value in monitoring parameters of health and longevity that we have some control over and can take action on if the testing indicates it is necessary. That said, testing costs money, and for the most part, so do longevity-based treatments. The one thing we can say for sure is that money spent on testing will not directly help your dog live better or longer. If there is a question of where to allocate finances, always prioritize treatment over diagnostics whenever possible.

Here are some guidelines to follow:

- Vaccines are necessary and beneficial, but overvaccination is dangerous. It is important to understand the risk-benefit analysis for all vaccines and medications.
- Ideally, spay or neuter dogs after they are fully physically mature. This means about one year for smaller dogs and as old as two or more years for giant breeds.
- Preventives like flea, tick, and heartworm medications have benefits, but they also have risks. Use them only at times when your dog is exposed. Have a heartworm test run annually if your dog is not on preventive every month.
- Pharmaceuticals such as antibiotics and anti-inflammatories are sometimes necessary, but they are overprescribed. Explore other options whenever possible.
- Regular examinations by your veterinarian can help detect medical problems early. Younger dogs should be seen at least once per year, while middle-aged or older dogs may benefit from two or three visits annually.
- Practice good oral health through regular dental care at home and, when necessary, with your veterinarian.
- Regular diagnostic testing in the form of blood, urine, and stool analysis is a valuable screening tool.
- Longevity-focused testing such as genetic screening, vitamin levels, inflammatory markers, and so forth provides great insight

into how to best implement longevity therapies in levels 4 and 5.

- Get pet insurance early so you never have to make major medical decisions based on cost.

LEVEL 4: SUPPLEMENTS

Diet, lifestyle, exercise, and thoughtful medical care are all critical components of your dog's longevity. As we move into supplements, we are entering a different realm of longevity science. We are leveraging our knowledge of the hallmarks of aging and strategically incorporating supplements to hack into our dogs' biology and allow their bodies to function better and longer. This is where things get really interesting . . .

Supplements for longevity are easily accessible and are generally very safe. Do your best to create a protocol that is both effective and sustainable on your end. Don't try to give your dog everything at once! There are combination supplements on the market that will allow you to check off multiple compounds on the list by giving a single product. This can make life a bit easier. Certain supplements, like omega fatty acids, are beneficial to give over the long term. Most others are better given for a period of time and then rotated out in exchange for different ones. This allows the body to benefit from accessing different pathways and mechanisms to positively affect the hallmarks of aging over time.

Here are some suggested guidelines for longevity supplementation:

Supplements you can give every day for the long term:

- Probiotics
    - These may include pre- and/or postbiotics.
    - Rotate through different products at least a few times annually.
- Omega fatty acids
    - Focus particularly on EPA and DHA found in marine oils.
    - If possible, check omega fatty acid levels through a blood test to ensure ideal levels of supplementation.
- Vitamins and minerals
    - Use formulas made for dogs, when available.
    - It's okay to rotate through different products over time to provide a spectrum of nutrients and sources of ingredients.
    - If your pet is eating a balanced, fresh-food diet, a multivitamin may not be necessary.

Rotation strategy for other supplements:

- The goal is to cover multiple hallmarks of aging with only a few supplements. The table on page 158 identifies which hallmarks each supplement addresses.
- Rotate supplements every one to two months.
- It is not necessary to use everything on the list.

- Keep it simple: Supplementing more than two or three things at any one time may become difficult to sustain, and/or your dog may not like it.

LEVEL 5: LONGEVITY-FOCUSED DRUGS AND MEDICAL THERAPIES

Accessibility and financial concerns are paramount when you consider longevity interventions at this level. When it comes to these kinds of treatments, always consult with a veterinarian before starting anything.

These therapies are changing the environment within your dog's body in ways that would otherwise be impossible. Having said that, these actions at the top of the pyramid require more of a financial commitment. While pet insurance generally will pay for treating a specific medical condition, they probably are not going to cover therapies being used to support longevity.

In addition to the cost considerations, many of the therapies and interventions described in Chapter 7 may not be readily available in your area. These are specialized therapies that, honestly, you would probably have a hard time finding if you needed to get *yourself* treated. If one or more of the treatments described is available for your dog, speak with the veterinarian providing the service about how your dog could best benefit.

To be clear, you can make an enormous impact on your dog's longevity without ever utilizing even one of these therapies, but I wanted to shine the light on every option that is currently available or forthcoming. As with everything else, whatever you do, it has to be sustainable for both you and your dog. I would much rather see people focus their efforts and resources toward feeding an optimal diet and creating an ideal lifestyle for their dog than spend all their money on high-tech interventions. You must establish the foundation for optimal health before you do anything else.

Here are some suggestions on how best to utilize these therapies if they are available to you:

- *Hyperbaric oxygen therapy:* While a study evaluating HBOT and telomere length in humans showed positive results, it required daily treatments for 60 days, and there has yet to be a veterinary-equivalent study. There is every reason to believe that HBOT benefits dogs the same way it does humans, and there are no drawbacks besides the potential cost. It may be possible for you to have your dog treated weekly or monthly for the long term, which might be helpful with supporting tissue repair and good health. Home-use hyperbaric chambers are available for purchase, but these are impractical because they pressurize with room air and require the user to wear an oxygen mask while in the chamber. In my experience, this is not something a dog will tolerate, so a chamber that pressurizes with oxygen, such as one found in a medical facility, will be necessary. Consult with a veterinarian familiar with HBOT to discuss the specific protocol.
- *Ozone therapy:* Ozone therapy at regular intervals is likely to provide health benefits for dogs. Ozone can be administered in a variety of ways, including via injection, through

ozonated water, and even rectally. If your veterinarian offers ozone, consider having your dog treated every four to eight weeks. Like HBOT, there are home units available for purchase that give ozone gas rectally. Some people do this for their own longevity, and you can provide it for your dog as well. Consult with a veterinarian familiar with ozone to discuss the specifics of how to do this safely for your dog.

- *Platelet-rich plasma:* PRP definitively requires a veterinarian, and generally I would only suggest it for the treatment of an injury, such as damage to a ligament, tendon, muscle, or joint.
- *Mesenchymal stem cell therapy:* Conventional stem cell therapy has applications in treating the same spectrum of injuries as PRP. As discussed in Chapter 7, the size of mesenchymal stem cells makes them impractical for IV administration, and thus they are not the best choice as an overall longevity therapy.
- *Very small embryonic-like stem cells:* VSELs are new to veterinary medicine and aren't even widely known in human medicine. The preliminary evidence we have so far indicates they can be used in the treatment of injuries like those mentioned above, as well as certain types of organ dysfunction like heart disease, brain and spinal cord conditions, and so forth. In addition, VSELs appear to be applicable as an overall longevity therapy, and anecdotally,

human patients who have been treated with VSELs have decreased their epigenetic ages as measured through DNA methylation. The originator of therapeutic VSELs, Dr. Todd Ovokaitys, treats his human patients quarterly to promote longevity. As of now, there are only a handful of veterinarians who are able to offer VSEL therapy for their patients. If you and your dog are in the San Francisco Bay Area, give me a call.

- *Microbiome restorative therapy:* MBRT, more commonly known as fecal transplantation, is typically used for patients with chronic GI issues, such as inflammatory bowel disease, colitis, dysbiosis, and so on. From a longevity perspective, there may be benefits to transplanting stool from a younger animal into an older one. This is the kind of thing that could be done once or twice annually. I probably don't have to say this, *but don't try this at home*. Donor animals should be carefully selected based on lifestyle, medication history, and diet, and their stool must be screened to ensure it is free of pathogens. Do this only through your veterinarian.
- *Rapamycin:* As pharmaceuticals go, rapamycin appears to have the greatest potential as a longevity drug, and there is ongoing research into its effects on dogs. Rapamycin should only be used intermittently, as long-term inhibition of the mTOR pathway is potentially

harmful. Administer this only under direct veterinary supervision.

- *Dasatinib:* Dasatinib is a potent senolytic and thus probably could be useful in an overall longevity plan, although it hasn't been researched for this purpose in dogs. Recall that dasatinib is also a chemotherapy drug, so don't take its use lightly. Like rapamycin, it should be used intermittently and only under direct veterinary supervision.
- *Peptides:* Peptides are exciting because they are a broad class of compounds that show a lot of potential to promote healing and longevity. In addition, they can be administered at home by pet owners. Depending on the peptide, they may be oral or injectable. As a rule, peptides are given in cycles and are frequently stacked, meaning that more than one peptide is given per cycle. Cycles generally last from one to three months. Even though this is something you can do at home, definitely consult with a veterinarian prior to implementing peptide therapy.

CONCLUSIONS . . . BUT NOT THE END

Before you started reading this book, you may have thought of aging as an unstoppable force. That would be understandable, since during the entire history of the world, that has been the case. With an understanding of the hallmarks of aging, however, we have shone a light onto mechanisms that can be used to stop the unstoppable.

Consider this: A little over 100 years ago, the concept of riding in a machine that can fly would have been considered ludicrous. Now millions of people fly every day. A little over 50 years ago, the idea of space travel was the stuff of H. G. Wells and other science-fiction writers. Now we have space tourism and asteroid mining. Things that once seemed impossible have a way of not only becoming possible but also unremarkable. Yesterday's miracles are today's mundane occurrences. Extending life span is just one more of these things.

The information provided in these chapters represents most of what current longevity science has to say and offer to people in search of longer and better lives for themselves and their dogs. As much information as was presented here, the field of longevity science is in its earliest stages. Renowned futurist Ray Kurzweil predicts human longevity will reach "escape velocity" by approximately 2030. This means we will be able to turn the clock back faster than we are chronologically aging. In other words, people—and presumably animals like dogs—will no longer have to age and may even be able to do so in reverse and get younger!

The best course of action right now is to utilize the information in this book to keep your dog as healthy and happy as possible. Create the best life you can for the both of you, and you may find you are able to extend your dog's quality and quantity of life. Depending on how old your dog is now, the two of you may reach escape velocity together!

RESOURCES

Lifespan: Why We Age—and Why We Don't Have To, by David Sinclair

Super Human: The Bulletproof Plan to Age Backward and Maybe Even Live Forever, by Dave Asprey

The Energy Formula: Six Life Changing Ingredients to Unleash Your Limitless Potential, by Shawn Wells

Why You Are Still Sick: How Infections Can Break Your Immune System & How You Can Recover, by Gary Kaplan and Donna Beech

The Ultimate Pet Health Guide: Breakthrough Nutrition and Integrative Care for Dogs and Cats, by Gary Richter

* * *

Ultimate Pet Nutrition: www.ultimatepetnutrition.com

ENDNOTES

Chapter 1

1. "Oldest dog ever," *Guinness Book of World Records,* January 10, 2023, http://www.guinnessworldrecords.com/world-records/oldest-dog.

2. M. Gannon, "China's first emperor ordered official search for immortality elixir," *Live Science,* December 27, 2017, https://www.livescience.com/61286-first-chinese-emperor-sought-immortality.html.

3. C. López-Otín et al., "The hallmarks of aging," *Cell* 153, no. 6 (June 6, 2013): 1194–217, https://www.ncbi.nlm.nih.gov/pmc/articles/PMC3836174.

4. T. Schmauck-Medina et al., "New hallmarks of ageing: a 2022 Copenhagen ageing meeting summary," *Aging* (Albany, NY) 14, no. 16 (August 29, 2022): 6829–39, https://doi.org/10.18632/aging.204248.

5. S. Horvath and K. Raj, "DNA methylation-based biomarkers and the epigenetic clock theory of ageing," *Nature Reviews Genetics* 19 (2018): 371–84, https://www.nature.com/articles/s41576-018-0004-3.

6. L. Fontana, L. Partridge, and V. D. Longo, "Extending healthy life span—from yeast to humans," *Science* 328, no. 5976 (April 16, 2010): 321–26.

7. D. Papadopoli et al., "mTOR as a central regulator of lifespan and aging," *F1000Research* 8 (July 2, 2019): F1000 Faculty Rev-998, https://www.ncbi.nlm.nih.gov/pmc/articles/PMC6611156.

8. T. Wilmanski et al., "Gut microbiome pattern reflects healthy ageing and predicts survival in humans," *Nature Metabolism* 3, no. 2 (February 2021): 274–86, https://doi.org/10.1038/s42255-021-00348-0.

9. *Merriam-Webster*, s.v. "disease (n.)," accessed June 15, 2022, https://www.merriam-webster.com/dictionary/disease.

Chapter 2

1. "The Human Genome Project," About Genomics, National Human Genome Research Institute, National Institutes of Health, Bethesda, MD, updated September 2, 2022, https://www.genome.gov/human-genome-project.

2. M. J. Berridge, "Vitamin D deficiency accelerates ageing and age-related diseases: a novel hypothesis," *Journal of Physiology* 595, no. 22 (2017): 6825–36, https://doi.org/10.1113/JP274887.

3. Z. Zou et al., "Magnesium in aging and aging-related disease," *STEMedicine* 3, no. 2 (2022): e119, https://doi.org/10.37175/stemedicine.v3i2.119.

4. E. E. Bitter et al., "Thymidine kinase 1 through the ages: a comprehensive review," *Cell & Bioscience* 10, no. 138 (November 27, 2020), https://doi.org/10.1186/s13578-020-00493-1.

5. M. I. McBurney et al., "Using an erythrocyte fatty acid fingerprint to predict risk of all-cause mortality: the Framingham Offspring Cohort," *American Journal of Clinical Nutrition* 114, no. 4 (2021): 1447–54, https://doi.org/10.1093/ajcn/nqab195.

6. A. D. Romano et al., "Oxidative stress and aging," *Journal of Nephrology* 23, suppl.15 (September–October 2010): S29–36.

7. W. J. Dodds, "Biomarkers of oxidative stress in dogs," *Medical Research Archives* 8, no. 5 (May 2020), https://esmed.org/MRA/mra/article/view/2112/193545570.

8. W. J. Dodds, "Diagnosis of feline food sensitivity and intolerance using saliva: 1000 cases," *Animals* (Basel) 9, no. 8 (August 6, 2019): 534, https://doi.org/10.3390/ani9080534.

9. S. P. Wiertsema et al., "The interplay between the gut microbiome and the immune system in the context of infectious diseases throughout life and the role of nutrition in optimizing treatment strategies," *Nutrients* 13, no. 3 (March 9, 2021): 886, https://doi.org/10.3390/nu13030886.

10. "Unique gut microbiome patterns linked to healthy aging, increased longevity," Research Highlights, National Institute on Aging, National Institutes of Health, Bethesda, MD, May 13, 2021, https://www.nia.nih.gov/news/unique-gut-microbiome-patterns-linked-healthy-aging-increased-longevity.

11. "Cancer in Pets," American Veterinary Medical Association, accessed June 15, 2022, https://www.avma.org/resources/pet-owners/petcare/cancer-pets#:~:text=How%20common%20are%20neoplasia%20and,rate%20of%20cancer%20in%20cats.

12. A. Flory et al., "Clinical validation of a next-generation sequencing-based multi-cancer early detection 'liquid biopsy' blood test in over 1,000 dogs using an independent testing set: the CANcer Detection in Dogs (CANDiD) study," *PLoS One* 17, no. 4 (2022): e0266623, https://journals.plos.org/plosone/article?id=10.1371/journal.pone.0266623.

13. E. A. Ostrander and R. K. Wayne, "The canine genome," *Genome Research* 15 (2005): 1706–16, https://genome.cshlp.org/content/15/12/1706.full#:~:text=The%20gene%20count%20of%20%E2%88%BC,dog%2C%20human%2C%20and%20mouse.

14. "What is a gene?," MedlinePlus, National Library of Medicine, updated March 22, 2021, https://medlineplus.gov/genetics/understanding/basics/gene/#:~:text=In%20humans%2C%20genes%20vary%20in,between%2020%2C000%20and%2025%2C000%20genes.

15. A. Vaiserman and D. Krasnienkov, "Telomere length as a marker of biological age: state-of-the-art, open issues, and future perspectives," *Frontiers in Genetics* 11 (January 21, 2021): 630186, https://doi.org/10.3389/fgene.2020.630186.

16. N. E. Braverman and A. B. Moser, "Functions of plasmalogen lipids in health and disease," *Biochimica et Biophysica Acta* 1822, no. 9 (September 2012): 1442–52, https://doi.org/10.1016/j.bbadis.2012.05.008.

17. Z. A. Almsherqi, "Potential role of plasmalogens in the modulation of biomembrane morphology," *Frontiers in Cell and Developmental Biology* (July 21, 2021), https://www.frontiersin.org/articles/10.3389/fcell.2021.673917/full.

18. X. Q. Su, J. Wang, and A. J. Sinclair, "Plasmalogens and Alzheimer's disease: a review," *Lipids in Health and Disease* 18, no. 100 (2019), https://doi.org/10.1186/s12944-019-1044-1.

19. I. Pradas et al., "Exceptional human longevity is associated with a specific plasma phenotype of ether lipids," *Redox Biology* 21 (2019): 101127, https://doi.org/10.1016/j.redox.2019.101127.

20. T. Kimura et al., "Plasmalogen loss caused by remodeling deficiency in mitochondria," *Life Science Alliance* 2, no. 4 (August 21, 2019): e201900348, https://doi.org/10.26508/lsa.201900348.

21. M. Raffaele and M. Vinciguerra, "The costs and benefits of senotherapeutics for human health," *Lancet Healthy Longevity* 3 (2022): e67–e77, https://www.thelancet.com/pdfs/journals/lanhl/PIIS2666-7568(21)00300-7.pdf.

22. R. J. Pignolo et al., "Reducing senescent cell burden in aging and disease," *Trends in Molecular Medicine* 26, no. 7 (July 2020): 630–38, https://doi.org/10.1016/j.molmed.2020.03.005.

Chapter 3

1. E. Yong, "A new origin story for dogs: the first domesticated animals may have been tamed twice," *The Atlantic*, June 2, 2016, https://www.theatlantic.com/science/archive/2016/06/the-origin-of-dogs/484976.

2. B. N. Ames, "Low micronutrient intake may accelerate the degenerative diseases of aging through allocation of scarce micronutrients by triage," *Proceedings of the National Academy of Sciences* 103, no. 47 (November 21, 2006): 17589–17594, https://www.pnas.org/doi/10.1073/pnas.0608757103.

3. C. Copat et al., "Heavy metals concentrations in fish and shellfish from eastern Mediterranean Sea: consumption advisories," *Food and Chemical Toxicology* 53 (March 2013): 33–37, https://doi.org/10.1016/j.fct.2012.11.038.

4. Z. Petrovic et al., "Meat production and consumption: environmental consequences," *Procedia Food Science* 5 (2015): 235–38, https://www.sciencedirect.com/science/article/pii/S2211601X15001315.

5. G. S. Okin, "Environmental impacts of food consumption by dogs and cats," *PLoS One* 12, no. 8 (2017): e0181301, https://journals.plos.org/plosone/article?id=10.1371/journal.pone.0181301.

6. J. L. Kaplan et al., "Taurine deficiency and dilated cardiomyopathy in golden retrievers fed commercial diets," *PLoS One* 13, no. 12 (December 13, 2018): e0209112, https://doi.org/10.1371/journal.pone.0209112.

7. T. Luntz, "U.S. drinking water widely contaminated," *Scientific American*, December 14, 2009, https://www.scientificamerican.com/article/tap-drinking-water-contaminants-pollutants.

8. E. Bedford, "U.S. pet market sales by category 2018–2021," *Statista*, September 8, 2022, https://www.statista.com/statistics/253983/pet-market-sales-in-the-us-by-category.

9. T. Wall, "Decade-long fresh, raw pet food sales growth trend," *PetFoodIndustry.com*, December 17, 2021, https://www.petfoodindustry.com/articles/10892-decade-long-fresh-raw-pet-food-sales-growth-trend?v=preview#:~:text=In%20Packaged%20Facts'%20most%20recent,U.S.%20pet%20food%20retail%20sales.

10. N. Tamanna and N. Mahmood, "Food processing and Maillard reaction products: effect on human health and nutrition," *International Journal of Food Science* 3 (2015): 1–6, https://doi.org/10.1155/2015/526762.

11. D. Schröter and A. Höhn, "Role of advanced glycation end products in carcinogenesis and their therapeutic implications," *Current Pharmaceutical Design* 24, no. 44 (2018): 5245–51, https://doi.org/10.2174/1381612825666190130145549.

12. G. Richter, *The Ultimate Pet Health Guide: Breakthrough Nutrition and Integrative Care for Dogs and Cats* (Carlsbad, CA: Hay House, 2017), 38.

13. R. Weindruch and R. S. Sohal, "Seminars in medicine of the Beth Israel Deaconess Medical Center. Caloric intake and aging," *New England Journal of Medicine* 337, no. 14 (1997): 986–94, https://doi.org/10.1056/NEJM199710023371407.

14. V. Adams et al., "Exceptional longevity and potential determinants of successful ageing in a cohort of 39 Labrador retrievers: results of a prospective longitudinal study," *Acta veterinaria Scandinavica* 58, no. 1 (May 11, 2016), https://doi.org/10.1186/s13028-016-0206-7.

15. A. K. Shetty et al., "Emerging anti-aging strategies—scientific basis and efficacy," *Aging and Disease* 9, no. 6 (December 4, 2018): 1165–84, https://www.ncbi.nlm.nih.gov/pmc/articles/PMC6284760.

16. E. E. Bray et al., "Once-daily feeding is associated with better health in companion dogs: results from the Dog Aging Project," *GeroScience* 44 (April 28, 2022): 1779–90, https://doi.org/10.1007/s11357-022-00575-7.

Chapter 4

1. H. R. Patil et al., "Cardiovascular damage resulting from chronic excessive endurance exercise," *Missouri Medicine* 109, no. 4 (July–August 2012): 312–21.

2. C. Salt et al., "Association between life span and body condition in neutered client-owned dogs," *Journal of Internal Veterinary Medicine* 33, no. 1 (December 11, 2018): 89–99, https://onlinelibrary.wiley.com/doi/10.1111/jvim.15367.

3. M. Venturelli, F. Schena, and R. S. F. Richardson, "The role of exercise capacity in the health and longevity of centenarians," *Maturitas* 73, no. 2 (October 2012): 115–20, https://doi.org/10.1016/j.maturitas.2012.07.009.

4. L. Mandolesi et al., "Effects of physical exercise on cognitive functioning and wellbeing: biological and psychological benefits," *Frontiers in Psychology* 9 (April 27, 2018): 509, https://doi.org/10.3389/fpsyg.2018.00509.

5. A. Rebelo-Marques et al., "Aging hallmarks: the benefits of physical exercise," *Frontiers in Endocrinology* (Lausanne) 9 (May 25, 2018): 258, https://doi.org/10.3389/fendo.2018.00258.

6. D. B. Walker et al., "Naturalistic quantification of canine olfactory sensitivity," *Applied Animal Behaviour Science* 97, no. 2–4 (2006): 241–54, https://doi.org/10.1016/j.applanim.2005.07.009.

7. E. R. Walker, R. E. McGee, and B. G. Druss, "Mortality in mental disorders and global disease burden implications: a systematic review and meta-analysis," *JAMA Psychiatry* 72, no. 4 (April 2015): 334–41, https://doi.org/10.1001/jamapsychiatry.2014.2502.

8. C. K. Chang et al., "Life expectancy at birth for people with serious mental illness and other major disorders from a secondary mental health care case register in London," *PLoS One* 6, no. 5 (May 18, 2011): e19590, https://doi.org/10.1371/journal.pone.0019590.

9. National Institute for Health and Welfare, cited in "Heavy stress and lifestyle can predict how long we live," ScienceDaily, March 11, 2020, https://www.sciencedaily.com/releases/2020/03/200311100857.htm#:~:text=Being%20under%20heavy%20stress%20shortens,expectancy%20of%20men%20and%20women.

10. A. Catarino et al., "Failing to forget: inhibitory-control deficits compromise memory suppression in posttraumatic stress disorder," *Psychological Science* 26, no. 5 (April 6, 2015): 604–16, https://doi.org/10.1177/0956797615569889.

11. "Caring for a dog with PTSD," VMBS News, School of Veterinary Medicine & Biomedical Sciences, Texas A&M University, July 16, 2020, https://vetmed.tamu.edu/news/pet-talk/caring-for-a-dog-with-ptsd.

12. B. L. Sherman and D. S. Mills, "Canine anxieties and phobias: an update on separation anxiety and noise aversions," *Veterinary Clinics of North America: Small Animal Practice* 38, no. 5 (September 2008): 1081–106, vii, https://doi.org/10.1016/j.cvsm.2008.04.012.

13. Dreschel, Nancy, "The effects of fear and anxiety on health and lifespan in pet dogs," *Applied Animal Behaviour Science* 125 (2010): 157 162, https://doi.org/ 10.1016/j.applanim.2010.04.003.

14. Y. Yu, B. Wilson, S. Masters, D. van Rooy, P. D. McGreevy, "Mortality Resulting from Undesirable Behaviours in Dogs Aged Three Years and under Attending Primary-Care Veterinary Practices in Australia," Animals 2021 Feb 13, 11(2): 493, https://doi.org 10.3390/ani11020493.

15. C. K. Kramer, S. Mehmood, and R. S. Suen, "Dog ownership and survival: a systematic review and meta-analysis," *Circulation: Cardiovascular Quality and Outcomes* 12, no. 10 (October 2019): e005554, https://doi.org/10.1161/CIRCOUTCOMES.119.005554.

16. E. Friedmann et al., "Pet ownership patterns and successful aging outcomes in community dwelling older adults," *Frontiers in Veterinary Science* 7 (June 25, 2020): 293, https://doi.org/10.3389/fvets.2020.00293.

17. "The happiness of pet owners: new study reveals the happiest pet owners," How To Be Happy, Case Studies & Surveys, Tracking Happiness, updated April 18, 2022, https://www.trackinghappiness.com/happiness-of-pet-owners-study.

18. L. O. Lee et al., "Optimism is associated with exceptional longevity in 2 epidemiologic cohorts of men and women," *Proceedings of the National Academy of Sciences* 116, no. 37 (September 10, 2019): 18357–62, https://doi.org/10.1073/pnas.1900712116.

Chapter 5

1. J. Jureidini and L. B. McHenry, "The illusion of evidence based medicine," *BMJ*, (March 2022): 376, https://doi.org/10.1136/bmj.o702.

2. D. L. Knobel et al., "Rabies vaccine is associated with decreased all-cause mortality in dogs," *Vaccine* 35, no. 31 (July 5, 2017): 3844–49, https://doi.org/10.1016/j.vaccine.2017.05.095.

3. W. J. Dodds et al., "Duration of immunity after rabies vaccination in dogs: The Rabies Challenge Fund research study," *Can J Vet Res* 84, no. 2 (April 2020): 153–8, https://pubmed.ncbi.nlm.nih.gov/32255911/.

4. Y. Shoenfeld and A. Aron-Maor, "Vaccination and autoimmunity-'vaccinosis': a dangerous liaison?" *J Autoimmun* 14, no. 1 (February 2000): 1–10, https://doi.org/10.1006/jaut.1999.0346.

5. P. Farhoody et al., "Aggression toward familiar people, strangers, and conspecifics in gonadectomized and intact dogs," *Frontiers in Veterinary Science* 5 (February 26, 2018): 18, https://doi.org/10.3389/fvets.2018.00018.

6. J. M. Hoffman, K. E. Creevy, and D. E. Promislow, "Reproductive capability is associated with lifespan and cause of death in companion dogs," *PLoS One* 8, no. 4 (April 17, 2013): e61082, https://doi.org/10.1371/journal.pone.0061082.

7. B. L. Hart et al., "Assisting decision-making on age of neutering for 35 breeds of dogs: associated joint disorders, cancers, and urinary incontinence," *Frontiers in Veterinary Science* 7 (July 7, 2020): 388, https://doi.org/10.3389/fvets.2020.00388.

8. L. M. T. Dicks, S. M. Deane, and M. J. Grobbelaar, "Could the COVID-19-driven increased use of ivermectin lead to incidents of imbalanced gut microbiota and dysbiosis?," *Probiotics and Antimicrobial Proteins* 14, no. 2 (April 2022): 217–23, https://doi.org/10.1007/s12602-022-09925-5.

9. M. Levy et al., "Dysbiosis and the immune system," *Nature Reviews Immunology* 17, no. 4 (April 2017): 219–32, https://doi.org/10.1038/nri.2017.7.

10. G. A. Weiss and T. Hennet, "Mechanisms and consequences of intestinal dysbiosis," *Cellular and Molecular Life Sciences* 74, no. 16 (August 2017): 2959–77, https://doi.org/10.1007/s00018-017-2509-x.

11. "Heartworm incidence maps," American Heartworm Society, https://www.heartwormsociety.org/veterinary-resources/incidence-maps.

12. S. R. Urfer et al., "Risk factors associated with lifespan in pet dogs evaluated in primary care veterinary hospitals," *Journal of the American Animal Hospital Association* 55, no. 3 (May/June 2019): 130–37, https://doi.org/10.5326/JAAHA-MS-6763.

13. Y. Watanabe et al., "Oral health for achieving longevity," *Geriatrics & Gerontology International* 20, no. 6 (June 2020): 526–38, https://doi.org/10.1111/ggi.13921.

14. Y. Heianza et al., "Duration and life-stage of antibiotic use and risks of all-cause and cause-specific mortality: prospective cohort study," *Circulation Research* 126, no. 3 (January 31, 2020): 364–73, https://doi.org/10.1161/CIRCRESAHA.119.315279.

15. C. He et al., "Enhanced longevity by ibuprofen, conserved in multiple species, occurs in yeast through inhibition of tryptophan import," *PLoS Genet* 10, no. 12 (December 18, 2014): e1004860, https://doi.org/10.1371/journal.pgen.1004860.

16. A. Danilov et al., "Influence of non-steroidal anti-inflammatory drugs on *Drosophila melanogaster* longevity," *Oncotarget* 6, no. 23 (August 14, 2015): 19428–44, https://doi.org/10.18632/oncotarget.5118.

Chapter 6

1. V. Raguraman and J. Subramaniam, "Withania somnifera root extract enhances telomerase activity in the human HeLa cell line," *Advances in Bioscience and Biotechnology* 7, no. 4 (April 2016), https://www.researchgate.net/publication/301295944_Withania_somnifera_Root_Extract_Enhances_Telomerase_Activity_in_the_Human_HeLa_Cell_Line.

2. R. Guo et al., "Withaferin A prevents myocardial ischemia/reperfusion injury by upregulating AMP-activated protein kinase-dependent B-cell lymphoma2 signaling," *Circulation Journal* 83, no. 8 (July 25, 2019): 1726–36, https://doi.org/10.1253/circj.CJ-18-1391.

3. S. Koduru et al., "Notch-1 inhibition by Withaferin-A: a therapeutic target against colon carcinogenesis," *Molecular Cancer Therapeutics* 9, no. 1 (2010): 202–10, https://doi.org/10.1158/1535-7163.MCT-09-0771.

4. M. F. McCarty, "AMPK activation—protean potential for boosting healthspan," *AGE* 36, no. 2 (April 2014): 641–63, https://doi.org/10.1007/s11357-013-9595-y.

5. Y. Dang et al., "Berberine ameliorates cellular senescence and extends the lifespan of mice via regulating p16 and cyclin protein expression," *Aging Cell* 19, no. 1 (2020): e13060, https://doi.org/10.1111/acel.13060.

6. S. Massimino et al., "Effects of age and dietary beta-carotene on immunological variables in dogs," *Journal of Veterinary Internal Medicine* 17, no. 6 (November–December 2003): 835–42, https://doi.org/10.1111/j.1939-1676.2003.tb02523.x.

7. T. Nordström et al., "Associations between circulating carotenoids, genomic instability and the risk of high-grade prostate cancer," *The Prostate* 76, no. 4 (2016): 339–48, https://doi.org/10.1002/pros.23125.

8. D. Mantle and I. Hargreaves, "Coenzyme Q10 and degenerative disorders affecting longevity: an overview," *Antioxidants* (Basel) 8, no. 2 (February 16, 2019): 44, https://doi.org/10.3390/antiox8020044.

9. J. D. Hernández-Camacho et al., "Coenzyme Q_{10} supplementation in aging and disease," *Frontiers in Physiology* 4, no. 44 (February 5, 2018), https://www.frontiersin.org/articles/10.3389/fphys.2018.00044/full.

10. P. Shinde et al., "Curcumin restores the engraftment capacity of aged hematopoietic stem cells and also reduces PD-1 expression on cytotoxic T cells," *Journal of Tissue Engineering and Regenerative Medicine* 15, no. 4 (April 2021): 388–400, https://doi.org/10.1002/term.3180.

11. Z. Yang et al., "Curcumin-mediated bone marrow mesenchymal stem cell sheets create a favorable immune microenvironment for adult full-thickness cutaneous wound healing," *Stem Cell Research & Therapy* 9, no. 1 (January 31, 2018): 21, https://doi.org/10.1186/s13287-018-0768-6.

12. F. Mottola et al., "DNA damage in human amniotic cells: antigenotoxic potential of curcumin and α-lipoic acid," *Antioxidants* (Basel) 10, no. 7 (July 7, 2021): 1137, https://doi.org/10.3390/antiox10071137.

13. R. Sharma et al., "Long-term consumption of green tea EGCG enhances murine healthspan by mitigating multiple aspects of cellular senescence in mitotic and post-mitotic tissues, gut dysbiosis, and immunosenescence," *The Journal of Nutritional Biochemistry* 107 (May 23, 2022): 109068, https://doi.org/10.1016/j.jnutbio.2022.109068.

14. L. G. Xiong et al., "Epigallocatechin-3-gallate promotes healthy lifespan through mitohormesis during early-to-mid adulthood in Caenorhabditis elegans," *Redox Biology* 14 (2018): 305–15, https://doi.org/10.1016/j.redox.2017.09.019.

15. L. Yang et al., "The epigenetic modification of epigallocatechin gallate (EGCG) on cancer," *Current Drug Targets* 21, no. 11 (2020): 1099–104, https://doi.org/10.2174/1389450121666200504080112.

16. H. Ding et al., "Epigallocatechin-3-gallate activates the AMP-activated protein kinase signaling pathway to reduce lipid accumulation in canine hepatocytes," *Journal of Cellular Physiology* 236, no. 1 (January 2021): 405–16, https://doi.org/10.1002/jcp.29869.

17. M. I. McBurney et al., "Using an erythrocyte fatty acid fingerprint to predict risk of all-cause mortality: the Framingham Offspring Cohort," *The American Journal of Clinical Nutrition* (October 2021): 1447–54, https://doi.org/10.1093/ajcn/nqab195.

18. R. Farzaneh-Far et al., "Association of marine omega-3 fatty acid levels with telomeric aging in patients with coronary heart disease," *JAMA* 303, no. 3 (2010): 250–57, https://doi.org/10.1001/jama.2009.2008.

19. C. M. Champigny et al., "Omega-3 monoacylglyceride effects on longevity, mitochondrial metabolism and oxidative stress: insights from *Drosophila melanogaster*," *Marine Drugs* 16, no. 11 (November 16, 2018): 453, https://doi.org/10.3390/md16110453.

20. U. N. Das, "'Cell membrane theory of senescence' and the role of bioactive lipids in aging, and aging associated diseases and their therapeutic implications," *Biomolecules* 11, no. 2 (February 8, 2021): 241, https://doi.org/10.3390/biom11020241.

21. F. Ponte et al., "Improvement of genetic stability in lymphocytes from Fanconi anemia patients through the combined effect of α-lipoic acid and N-acetylcysteine," *Orphanet Journal of Rare Diseases* 7 (May 16, 2012): 28, https://doi.org/10.1186/1750-1172-7-28.

22. Mottola et al., "DNA damage in human amniotic cells."

23. S. M. Dos Santos et al., "Mitochondrial dysfunction and alpha-lipoic acid: beneficial or harmful in Alzheimer's disease?," *Oxidative Medicine and Cellular Longevity* 2019 (November 30, 2019): 8409329, https://doi.org/10.1155/2019/8409329.

24. M. J. Yousefzadeh et al., "Fisetin is a senotherapeutic that extends health and lifespan," *eBioMedicine* 36 (October 2018): 18–28, https://doi.org/10.1016/j.ebiom.2018.09.015.

25. Z. Zou et al., "Magnesium in aging and aging-related disease," *STEMedicine* 3, no. 2 (2022): e119, https://doi.org/10.37175/stemedicine.v3i2.119.

26. G. A. Bubenik and S. J. Konturek, "Melatonin and aging: prospects for human treatment," *Journal of Physiology and Pharmacology* 62, no. 1 (February 2011): 13–19, https://pubmed.ncbi.nlm.nih.gov/21451205.

27. J. Fang et al., "Melatonin prevents senescence of canine adipose-derived mesenchymal stem cells through activating NRF2 and inhibiting ER stress," *Aging* 10, no. 10 (2018): 2954–72, https://doi.org/10.18632/aging.101602.

28. H. H. Peng et al., "*Ganoderma lucidum* stimulates autophagy-dependent longevity pathways in *Caenorhabditis elegans* and human cells," *Aging* 13, no. 10 (2021): 13474–95, https://doi.org/10.18632/aging.203068.

29. D. M. Ba et al., "Association of mushroom consumption with all-cause and cause-specific mortality among American adults: prospective cohort study findings from NHANES III," *Nutrition Journal* 20, no. 1 (April 22, 2021): 38, https://doi.org/10.1186/s12937-021-00691-8.

30. Z. A. Hamid et al., "The role of N-acetylcysteine supplementation on the oxidative stress levels, genotoxicity and lineage commitment potential of ex vivo murine haematopoietic stem/progenitor cells," *Sultan Qaboos University Medical Journal* 18, no. 2 (May 2018): e130–e136, https://doi.org/10.18295/squmj.2018.18.02.002.

31. D. J. Wright et al., "N-Acetylcysteine improves mitochondrial function and ameliorates behavioral deficits in the R6/1 mouse model of Huntington's disease," *Translational Psychiatry* 5, no. 1 (January 6, 2015): e492, https://doi.org/10.1038/tp.2014.131.

32. C. Shade, "The science behind NMN-A stable, reliable NAD+activator and anti-aging molecule," *Integrative Medicine* (Encinitas, CA) 19, no. 1 (February 2020): 12–14.

33. Tokushima University and Nature Research Custom Media, "Recent research into nicotinamide mononucleotide and ageing," Sponsor Feature, Nature Portfolio, https://www.nature.com/articles/d42473-022-00002-7.

34. S. Rigacci et al., "Oleuropein aglycone induces autophagy via the AMPK/mTOR signalling pathway: a mechanistic insight," *Oncotarget* 6, no. 34 (November 3, 2015): 35344–57, https://doi.org/10.18632/oncotarget.6119.

35. K. Cuanalo-Contreras and I. Moreno-Gonzalez, "Natural products as modulators of the proteostasis machinery: implications in neurodegenerative diseases," *International Journal of Molecular Sciences* 20, no. 19 (September 20, 2019): 4666, https://doi.org/10.3390/ijms20194666.

36. X. Q. Su, J. Wang, and A. J. Sinclair, "Plasmalogens and Alzheimer's disease: a review," *Lipids in Health and Disease* 18, no. 1 (April 16, 2019): 100, https://doi.org/10.1186/s12944-019-1044-1.

37. M. S. Hossain, S. Mawatari, and T. Fujino, "Biological functions of plasmalogens," *Advances in Experimental Medicine and Biology* 1299 (2020): 171–93, https://doi.org/10.1007/978-3-030-60204-8_13.

38. Z. A. Almsherqi, "Potential role of plasmalogens in the modulation of biomembrane morphology," *Frontiers in Cell and Developmental Biology* 9 (July 21, 2021): 673917, https://doi.org/10.3389/fcell.2021.673917.

39. X. Fang et al., "Evaluation of the anti-aging effects of a probiotic combination isolated from centenarians in a SAMP8 mouse model," *Frontiers in Immunology* 12 (December 2, 2021): 792746, https://doi.org/10.3389/fimmu.2021.792746.

40. W. L. Teng et al., "Pterostilbene attenuates particulate matter-induced oxidative stress, inflammation and aging in keratinocytes," *Antioxidants* (Basel) 10, no. 10 (September 29, 2021): 1552, https://doi.org/10.3390/antiox10101552.

41. K. W. Lange and S. Li, "Resveratrol, pterostilbene, and dementia," *BioFactors* 44, no. 1 (January 2018): 83–90, https://doi.org/10.1002/biof.1396.

42. J. M. Suárez-Rivero et al., "Pterostilbene in combination with mitochondrial cofactors improve mitochondrial function in cellular models of mitochondrial diseases," *Frontiers in Pharmacology* 13 (March 18, 2022): 862085, https://doi.org/10.3389/fphar.2022.862085.

43. T. Simpson, C. Kure, and C. Stough, "Assessing the efficacy and mechanisms of Pycnogenol® on cognitive aging from in vitro animal and human studies," *Frontiers in Pharmacology* 10 (July 3, 2019): 694, https://doi.org/10.3389/fphar.2019.00694.

44. P. Rohdewald, "Pleiotropic effects of French maritime pine bark extract to promote healthy aging," *Rejuvenation Research* 22, no. 3 (June 2019): 210–17, https://doi.org/10.1089/rej.2018.2095.

45. Z. H. Wei, Q. L. Peng, and B. H. Lau, "Pycnogenol enhances endothelial cell antioxidant defenses," *Redox Report* 3, no. 4 (August 1997): 219–24, https://doi.org/10.1080/13510002.1997.11747113.

46. M. Hosoi et al., "Pycnogenol® supplementation in minimal cognitive dysfunction," *Journal of Neurosurgical Sciences* 62, no. 3 (June 2018): 279–84, https://doi.org/10.23736/S0390-5616.18.04382-5.

47. E. J. Sohn et al., "Restoring effects of natural anti-oxidant quercetin on cellular senescent human dermal fibroblasts," *The American Journal of Chinese Medicine* 46, no. 4 (2018): 853–73, https://doi .org/10.1142/S0192415X18500453.

48. K. Cuanalo-Contreras and I. Moreno-Gonzalez, "Natural products as modulators of the proteostasis machinery: implications in neurodegenerative diseases," *International Journal of Molecular Sciences* 20, no. 19 (September 20, 2019): 4666, https://doi .org/10.3390/ijms20194666.

49. E. J. Novais et al., "Long-term treatment with senolytic drugs Dasatinib and Quercetin ameliorates age-dependent intervertebral disc degeneration in mice," *Nature Communications* 12, no. 1 (September 3, 2021): 5213, https://doi.org/10.1038/ s41467-021-25453-2.

50. L. J. Hickson et al., "Senolytics decrease senescent cells in humans: preliminary report from a clinical trial of Dasatinib plus Quercetin in individuals with diabetic kidney disease," *eBioMedicine* 47 (September 2019): 446–56, https://doi.org/10.1016/j .ebiom.2019.08.069.

51. Y. R. Li, S. Li, and C. C. Lin, "Effect of resveratrol and pterostilbene on aging and longevity," *BioFactors* 44, no. 1 (January 2018): 69–82, https://doi.org/10.1002/biof.1400.

52. I. S. Pyo et al., "Mechanisms of aging and the preventive effects of resveratrol on age-related diseases," *Molecules* 25, no. 20 (October 12, 2020): 4649, https://doi.org/10.3390/molecules25204649.

53. D. D. Zhou et al., "Effects and mechanisms of resveratrol on aging and age-related diseases," *Oxidative Medicine and Cellular Longevity* 2021 (July 11, 2021): 9932218, https://doi.org/10.1155/2021/9932218.

54. "Selenium," The Nutrient Source, Harvard T. H. Chan School of Public Health, Harvard University, accessed 15 June 2022, https://www.hsph.harvard.edu/nutritionsource/selenium/#:~:text=Selenium%20is%20an%20essential%20component,the%20metabolism%20of%20thyroid%20hormones.

55. L. R. Ferguson et al., "Selenium and its role in the maintenance of genomic stability," *Mutation Research* 733, nos. 1–2 (May 1, 2012): 100–10, https://pubmed.ncbi.nlm.nih.gov/22234051.

56. Q. Wu et al., "Serine and metabolism regulation: a novel mechanism in antitumor immunity and senescence," *Aging and Disease* 11, no. 6 (December 1, 2020): 1640–53, https://doi.org/10.14336/AD.2020.0314.

57. R. A. Dunlop et al., "Mechanisms of L-serine neuroprotection in vitro include ER proteostasis regulation," *Neurotoxicity Research* 33, no. 1 (January 2018): 123–32, https://doi.org/10.1007/s12640-017-9829-3.

58. Dunlop et al., "Mechanisms of L-serine neuroprotection."

59. F. Madeo et al., "Spermidine delays aging in humans," *Aging* (Albany, NY) 10, no. 8 (2018): 2209–11, https://doi.org/10.18632/aging.101517.

60. F. Madeo et al., "Spermidine: a physiological autophagy inducer acting as an anti-aging vitamin in humans?" *Autophagy* 15, no. 1 (2019): 165–68, https://doi.org/10.1080/15548627.2018.1530929.

61. R. Santín-Márquez et al., "Sulforaphane—role in aging and neurodegeneration," *GeroScience* 41, no. 5 (2019): 655–70, https://doi.org/10.1007/s11357-019-00061-7.

62. S. F. Kan, J. Wang, and G. X. Sun, "Sulforaphane regulates apoptosis- and proliferation-related signaling pathways and synergizes with cisplatin to suppress human ovarian cancer," *International Journal of Molecular Medicine* 42, no. 5 (2018): 2447–58, https://doi.org/10.3892/ijmm.2018.3860.

63. A. T. Lam et al., "Oral vitamin A as an adjunct treatment for canine sebaceous adenitis," *Veterinary Dermatology* 22, no. 4 (August 2011): 305–11, https://doi.org/10.1111/j.1365-3164.2010.00944.x.

64. K. Mikkelsen and V. Apostolopoulos, "B vitamins and ageing," *Subcellular Biochemistry* 90 (2018): 451–70, https://doi.org/10.1007/978-981-13-2835-0_15.

65. F. Monacelli et al., "Vitamin C, aging and Alzheimer's disease," *Nutrients* 9 no. 7 (June 27, 2017): 670, https://doi.org/10.3390/nu9070670.

66. S. Mumtaz et al., "Aging and its treatment with vitamin C: a comprehensive mechanistic review," *Molecular Biology Reports* 48, no. 12 (December 2021): 8141–53, https://doi.org/10.1007/s11033-021-06781-4.

67. B. Abiri and M. Vafa, "Vitamin D and muscle sarcopenia in aging," *Methods in Molecular Biology* 2138 (2020): 29–47, https://doi.org/10.1007/978-1-0716-0471-7_2.

68. C. Aranow, "Vitamin D and the immune system," *Journal of Investigative Medicine* 59, no. 6 (2011): 881–86, https://doi.org/10.2310/JIM.0b013e31821b8755.

69. H. Godman, "Vitamin D supplements may reduce risk of invasive cancer," Harvard Health, Harvard Medical School, June 1, 2021, https://www.health.harvard.edu/cancer/vitamin-d-supplements-may-reduce-risk-of-invasive-cancer.

70. M. Zarei et al., "The relationship between vitamin D and telomere/telomerase: a comprehensive review," *The Journal of Frailty & Aging* 10, no. 1 (2021): 2–9, https://doi.org/10.14283/jfa.2020.33.

71. S. Sirajudeen, I. Shah, and A. Al Menhali, "A narrative role of vitamin D and its receptor: with current evidence on the gastric tissues," *International Journal of Molecular Sciences* 20, no. 15 (August 5, 2019): 3832, https://doi.org/10.3390/ijms20153832.

72. Q. Zhang et al., "Evaluation of common genetic variants in vitamin E-related pathway genes and colorectal cancer susceptibility," *Archives of Toxicology* 95, no. 7 (July 2021): 2523–32, https://doi.org/10.1007/s00204-021-03078-0.

73. U. Mabalirajan et al., "Effects of vitamin E on mitochondrial dysfunction and asthma features in an experimental allergic murine model," *Journal of Applied Physiology* 107, no. 4 (October 1, 2009): 1285–92, https://doi.org/10.1152/japplphysiol.00459.2009.

74. G. La Fata, P. Weber, and M. H. Mohajeri, "Effects of vitamin E on cognitive performance during ageing and in Alzheimer's disease," *Nutrients* 6, no. 12 (November 28, 2014): 5453–72, https://doi.org/10.3390/nu6125453.

75. M. Rhouma et al., "Anti-inflammatory response of dietary vitamin E and its effects on pain and joint structures during early stages of surgically induced osteoarthritis in dogs," *Canadian Journal of Veterinary Research* 77, no. 3 (July 2013): 191–98.

76. G. K., Schwalfenberg, "Vitamins K1 and K2: the emerging group of vitamins required for human health," *Journal of Nutrition and Metabolism* 2017 (June 18, 2017): 6254836, https://doi.org/10.1155/2017/6254836.

77. D. C. Simes et al., "Vitamin K as a powerful micronutrient in aging and age-related diseases: pros and cons from clinical studies," *International Journal of Molecular Sciences* 20, no. 17 (August 25, 2019): 4150, https://doi.org/10.3390/ijms20174150.

78. D. S. Popa, G. Bigman, and M. E. Rusu, "The role of vitamin K in humans: implication in aging and age-associated diseases," *Antioxidants* (Basel) 10, no. 4 (April 6, 2021): 566, https://doi.org/10.3390/antiox10040566.

79. Á. J. R. Cabrera, "Zinc, aging, and immunosenescence: an overview," *Pathobiology of Aging & Age-Related Diseases* 5, no. 1 (February 5, 2015): 25592, https://doi.org/10.3402/pba.v5.25592.

80. X. Yang et al., "Zinc enhances the cellular energy supply to improve cell motility and restore impaired energetic metabolism in a toxic environment induced by OTA," *Scientific Reports* 7, no, 1 (November 7, 2017): 14669, https://doi.org/10.1038/s41598-017-14868-x.

Chapter 7

1. C. K. Sen, "Wound healing essentials: let there be oxygen," *Wound Repair and Regeneration* 17, no. 1 (January–February 2009): 1–18, https://doi.org/10.1111/j.1524-475X.2008.00436.x.

2. A. Valli, A. L. Harris, and B. M. Kessler, "Hypoxia metabolism in ageing," *Aging* (Albany, NY) 7, no. 7 (July 2015): 465–66, https://doi.org/10.18632/aging.100782.

3. S. M. Welford and A. J. Giaccia, "Hypoxia and senescence: the impact of oxygenation on tumor suppression," *Molecular Cancer Research* 9, no. 5 (May 2011): 538–44, https://doi.org/10.1158/1541-7786.MCR-11-0065.

4. A. Simpson, "Compressed air as a therapeutic agent in the treatment of consumption, asthma, chronic bronchitis and other diseases," *Glasgow Medical Journal* 5, no. 17 (1857): 94–96.

5. S. Tejada et al., "Therapeutic effects of hyperbaric oxygen in the process of wound healing," *Current Pharmaceutical Design* 25, no. 15 (2019): 1682–93, https://doi.org/10.2174/138161282566619070316 2648.

6. B. B. Hart, "Hyperbaric oxygen for refractory osteomyelitis," *Undersea & Hyperbaric Medicine* 48, no. 3 (third quarter 2021): 297–321.

7. Q. Z. Lu et al., "Further application of hyperbaric oxygen in prostate cancer," *Medical Gas Research* 8, no. 4 (January 9, 2019): 167–71, https://doi.org/10.4103/2045-9912.248268.

8. I. Moen and L. E. B. Stuhr, "Hyperbaric oxygen therapy and cancer—a review," *Targeted Oncology* 7, no. 4 (December 2012): 233–42, https://doi.org/10.1007/s11523-012-0233-x.

9. S. Y. Chen et al., "Hyperbaric oxygen suppressed tumor progression through the improvement of tumor hypoxia and induction of tumor apoptosis in A549-cell-transferred lung cancer," *Scientific Reports* 11, no. 1 (June 8, 2021): 12033, https://doi.org/10.1038/s41598-021-91454-2.

10. Y. Hachmo et al., "Hyperbaric oxygen therapy increases telomere length and decreases immunosenescence in isolated blood cells: a prospective trial," *Aging* (Albany, NY) 12, no. 22 (November 18, 2020): 22445–56, https://doi.org/10.18632/aging.202188.

11. I. Peña-Villalobos et al., "Hyperbaric oxygen increases stem cell proliferation, angiogenesis and wound-healing ability of WJ-MSCs in diabetic mice," *Frontiers in Physiology* 9 (July 30, 2018): 995, https://doi.org/10.3389/fphys.2018.00995.

12. A. Hadanny et al., "Hyperbaric oxygen therapy induces transcriptome changes in elderly: a prospective trial," *Aging* (Albany, NY) 13, no. 22 (November 24, 2021): 24511–23, https://doi .org/10.18632/aging.203709.

13. A. Hadanny et al., "Cognitive enhancement of healthy older adults using hyperbaric oxygen: a randomized controlled trial," *Aging* (Albany, NY) 12, no. 13 (June 26, 2020): 13740–61, https://doi .org/10.18632/aging.103571.

14. F. J. Hidalgo-Tallón et al., "Updated review on ozone therapy in pain medicine," *Frontiers in Physiology* 13 (February 23, 2022): 840623, https://doi.org/10.3389/fphys.2022.840623.

15. N. L. Smith et al., "Ozone therapy: an overview of pharmacodynamics, current research, and clinical utility," *Medical*

Gas Research 7, no. 3 (October 17, 2017): 212–19, https://doi .org/10.4103/2045-9912.215752.

16. C. Scassellati et al., "Ozone: a natural bioactive molecule with antioxidant property as potential new strategy in aging and in neurodegenerative disorders," *Ageing Research Reviews* 63 (November 2020): 101138, https://doi.org/10.1016/j.arr.2020.101138.

17. S. Tang et al., "Ozone induces BEL7402 cell apoptosis by increasing reactive oxygen species production and activating JNK," *Annals of Translational Medicine* 9, no. 15 (August 2021): 1257, https://doi .org/10.21037/atm-21-3233.

18. B. Clavo et al., "Ozone therapy as adjuvant for cancer treatment: is further research warranted?," *Evidence-Based Complementary and Alternative Medicine* 2018 (September 9, 2018): 7931849, https://doi .org/10.1155/2018/7931849.

19. Hidalgo-Tallón et al., "Updated review on ozone therapy."

20. Smith et al., "Ozone therapy."

21. Scassellati et al., "Ozone: a natural bioactive molecule."

22. Clavo et al., "Ozone therapy as adjuvant."

23. Tang et al., "Ozone induces BEL7402 cell apoptosis."

24. Clavo et al., "Ozone therapy as adjuvant."

25. K. Sharun et al., "Therapeutic potential of platelet-rich plasma in canine medicine," *Archives of Razi Institute* 76, no. 4 (September–October 2021): 721–30, https://doi.org/10.22092/ ari.2021.355953.1749.

26. *Encyclopaedia Britannica Online*, s.v. "capillary," updated July 23, 2019, https://www.britannica.com/science/capillary.

27. E. Eggenhofer et al., "Mesenchymal stem cells are short-lived and do not migrate beyond the lungs after intravenous infusion," *Frontiers in Immunology* 3 (September 26, 2012): 297, https://doi.org/10.3389/ fimmu.2012.00297.

28. E. Bari et al., "Mesenchymal stem/stromal cell secretome for lung regeneration: the long way through 'pharmaceuticalization' for the best formulation," *Journal of Controlled Release* 309 (September 10, 2019): 11–24, https://doi.org/10.1016/j.jconrel.2019.07.022.

29. D. M. L. W. Kruk, "Mesenchymal stromal cells to regenerate emphysema: on the horizon?," *Respiration* 96, no. 2 (2018): 148–58, https://doi.org/10.1159/000488149.

30. M. Z. Ratajczak et al., "Very small embryonic-like (VSEL) stem cells: purification from adult organs, characterization, and biological significance," *Stem Cell Reviews* 4, no. 2 (summer 2008): 89–99, https://doi.org/10.1007/s12015-008-9018-0.

31. M. Z. Ratajczak, J. Ratajczak, and M. Kucia, "Very small embryonic-like stem cells (VSELs): an update and future directions," *Circulation Research* 124, no. 2 (January 17, 2019), https://www.ahajournals.org/doi/10.1161/CIRCRESAHA.118.314287#:~:text=Evidence%20has%20accumulated%20that%20VSELs,cells%2C%20and%20endothelial%20progenitor%20cells.

32. Ratajczak, Ratajczak, and Kucia, "Very small embryonic-like stem cells (VSELs)."

33. P. Hollands, D. R. Aboyeji, and T. Ovokaitys, "The action of modulated laser light on Human Very Small Embryonic-Like (hVSEL) stem cells in Platelet Rich Plasma (PRP)," *CellR4* 8 (2020): e2990, https://doi.org/10.32113/cellr4_202012_2990.

34. J. Brindley, P. Hollands, and T. Ovokaitys, "A theoretical mechanism for the action of SONG-modulated laser light on Human Very Small Embryonic-Like (hVSEL) stem cells in Platelet Rich Plasma (PRP)," *CellR4* 9 (2021): e3201, https://doi.org/10.32113/cellr4_20216_3201.

35. E. K. Zuba-Surma et al., "Very small embryonic-like stem cells: biology and therapeutic potential for heart repair," *Antioxidant & Redox Signaling* 15, no. 7 (October 1, 2011): 1821–34, https://doi.org/10.1089/ars.2010.3817.

36. M. Z. Ratajczak et al., "Very small embryonic-like (VSEL) stem cells in adult organs and their potential role in rejuvenation of tissues and longevity," *Experimental Gerontology* 43, no. 11 (November 2008): 1009–17, https://doi.org/10.1016/j.exger.2008.06.002.

37. P. Han et al., "The association between intestinal bacteria and allergic diseases—cause or consequence?," *Frontiers in Cellular and Infection Microbiology* 11 (April 15, 2021): 650893, https://doi.org/10.3389/fcimb.2021.650893.

38. K. L. Tooley, "Effects of the human gut microbiota on cognitive performance, brain structure and function: a narrative review," *Nutrients* 12, no. 10 (September 30, 2020): 3009, https://doi.org/10.3390/nu12103009.

39. J. Liu et al., "Gut microbiota approach—a new strategy to treat Parkinson's disease," *Frontiers in Cellular and Infection Microbiology* 10 (October 22, 2020): 570658, https://doi.org/10.3389/fcimb.2020.570658.

40. O. C. Aroniadis and L. J. Brandt, "Intestinal microbiota and the efficacy of fecal microbiota transplantation in gastrointestinal disease," *Gastroenterology & Hepatology* 10, no. 4 (April 2014): 230–37.

41. "Fecal transplants restore gut microbes after antibiotics," NIH Research Matters, National Institutes of Health, Bethesda, MD, October 16, 2018, https://www.nih.gov/news-events/nih-research-matters/fecal-transplants-restore-gut-microbes-after-antibiotics.

42. A. Parker et al., "Fecal microbiota transfer between young and aged mice reverses hallmarks of the aging gut, eye, and brain," *Microbiome* 10, no. 1 (April 29, 2022): 618, https://doi.org/10.1186/s40168-022-01243-w.

43. M. J. Conboy, I. M. Conboy, and T. A. Rando, "Heterochronic parabiosis: historical perspective and methodological considerations for studies of aging and longevity," *Aging Cell* 12, no. 3 (June 2013): 525–30, https://doi.org/10.1111/acel.12065.

44. M. Mehdipour et al., "Rejuvenation of three germ layers tissues by exchanging old blood plasma with saline-albumin," *Aging* (Albany, NY) 12, no. 10 (May 30, 2020): 8790–819, https://doi.org/10.18632/aging.103418.

45. M. Mehdipour et al., "Plasma dilution improves cognition and attenuates neuroinflammation in old mice," *GeroScience* 43, no. 1 (February 2021): 1–18, https://doi.org/10.1007/s11357-020-00297-8.

46. M. V. Blagosklonny, "Rapamycin for longevity: opinion article," *Aging* (Albany, NY) 11, no. 19 (October 4, 2019): 8048–67, https://doi.org/10.18632/aging.102355.

47. R. Selvarani, S. Mohammed, and A. Richardson, "Effect of rapamycin on aging and age-related diseases—past and future," *GeroScience* 43, no. 3 (June 2021): 1135–58, https://doi.org/10.1007/s11357-020-00274-1.

48. "Dog Aging Project goal is to help both dogs and humans live longer, healthier lives," National Institute on Aging, National Institutes of Health, Bethesda, MD, February 24, 2022, https://www.nia.nih.gov/news/dog-aging-project-goal-help-both-dogs-and-humans-live-longer-healthier-lives.

49. C. López-Otín et al., "The hallmarks of aging," *Cell* 153, no. 6 (June 6, 2013): 1194–217, https://doi.org/10.1016/j.cell.2013.05.039.

50. S. Zeng, W. H. Shen, and L. Liu, "Senescence and cancer," *Cancer Translational Medicine* 4, no. 3 (May–June 2018): 70–74, https://pubmed.ncbi.nlm.nih.gov/30766922.

51. M. Xu et al., "Senolytics improve physical function and increase lifespan in old age," *Nature Medicine* 24, no. 8 (August 2018): 1246–56, https://doi.org/10.1038/s41591-018-0092-9.

52. M. B. Cavalcante et al., "Dasatinib plus quercetin prevents uterine age-related dysfunction and fibrosis in mice," *Aging* (Albany, NY) 12, no. 3 (January 18, 2020): 2711–22, https://doi.org/10.18632/aging.102772.

53. E. J. Novais et al., "Long-term treatment with senolytic drugs Dasatinib and Quercetin ameliorates age-dependent intervertebral disc degeneration in mice," *Nature Communications* 12, no. 1 (September 3, 2021): 5213, https://doi.org/10.1038/s41467-021-25453-2.

54. J. L. Kirkland and T. Tchkonia, "Senolytic drugs: from discovery to translation," *Journal of Internal Medicine* 288, no. 5 (November 2020): 518–36, https://doi.org/10.1111/joim.13141.

55. S. Seiwerth et al., "Stable gastric pentadecapeptide BPC 157 and wound healing," *Frontiers in Pharmacology* 12 (June 29, 2021): 627533, https://doi.org/10.3389/fphar.2021.627533.

56. D. Gwyer, N. M. Wragg, and S. L. Wilson, "Gastric pentadecapeptide body protection compound BPC 157 and its role in accelerating musculoskeletal soft tissue healing," *Cell and Tissue Research* 377, no. 2 (August 2019): 153–59, https://doi.org/10.1007/s00441-019-03016-8.

57. P. Sikiric, "Brain-gut axis and pentadecapeptide BPC 157: theoretical and practical implications," *Current Neuropharmacology* 14, no. 8 (2016): 857–65, https://doi.org/10.2174/1570159x13666160502153022.

58. A. L. Goldstein et al., "Thymosin β4: a multi-functional regenerative peptide. Basic properties and clinical applications," *Expert Opinion on Biological Therapy* 12, no. 1 (January 2012): 37–51, https://doi.org/10.1517/14712598.2012.634793.

59. G. T. Pipes and J. Yang, "Cardioprotection by thymosin beta 4," *Vitamins and Hormones* 102 (2016): 209–26, https://doi.org/10.1016/bs.vh.2016.04.004.

60. G. Sosne, "Thymosin beta 4 and the eye: the journey from bench to bedside," *Expert Opinion on Biological Therapy* 18, suppl. 1 (2018): 99–104, https://doi.org/10.1080/14712598.2018.1486818.

61. J. Kim and Y. Jung, "Thymosin beta 4 is a potential regulator of hepatic stellate cells," *Vitamins and Hormones* 102 (2016): 121–49, https://doi.org/10.1016/bs.vh.2016.04.011.

62. K. Maar et al., "Utilizing developmentally essential secreted peptides such as thymosin beta-4 to remind the adult organs of their embryonic state—new directions in anti-aging regenerative therapies," *Cells* 10, no. 6 (May 28, 2021): 1343, https://doi.org/10.3390/cells10061343.

63. Y. Zhang et al., "Thymosin Beta 4 is overexpressed in human pancreatic cancer cells and stimulates proinflammatory cytokine secretion and JNK activation," *Cancer Biology & Therapy* 7, no. 3 (March 2008): 419–23, https://doi.org/10.4161/cbt.7.3.5415.

64. J. Caers et al., "Thymosin β4 has tumor suppressive effects and its decreased expression results in poor prognosis and decreased survival in multiple myeloma," *Haematologica* 95, no. 1 (January 2010): 163–67, https://doi.org/10.3324/haematol.2009.006411.

65. G. Sosne and H. K. Kleinman, "Primary mechanisms of thymosin β4 repair activity in dry eye disorders and other tissue injuries," *Investigative Ophthalmology & Visual Science* 56, no. 9 (August 2015): 5110–17, https://doi.org/10.1167/iovs.15-16890.

66. S. L. Teichman et al., "Prolonged stimulation of growth hormone (GH) and insulin-like growth factor I secretion by CJC-1295, a long-acting analog of GH-releasing hormone, in healthy adults," *The Journal of Clinical Endocrinology & Metabolism* 91, no. 3 (March 2006): 799–805, https://doi.org/10.1210/jc.2005-1536.

67. M. Alba et al., "Once-daily administration of CJC-1295, a long-acting growth hormone-releasing hormone (GHRH) analog, normalizes growth in the GHRH knockout mouse," *AJP Endocrinology and Metabolism* 291, no. 6 (December 2006): e1290–4, https://doi.org/10.1152/ajpendo.00201.2006.

68. K. Raun et al., "Ipamorelin, the first selective growth hormone secretagogue," *European Journal of Endocrinology* 139, no. 5 (November 1998): 552–61, https://pubmed.ncbi.nlm.nih.gov/9849822.

INDEX

NOTE: Page references in *italics* refer to figures.

A

B

C

D

E

F

G

H

L

M

N

O

P

U

V

W

Y

Z

ACKNOWLEDGMENTS

Support in writing this book came from multiple sources, including some of the world's leading longevity physicians: Dr. Jeffery Gladden, Dr. Todd Ovokaitys, Dr. Matthew Cook, and Dr. Harry McIlroy. Thanks also to Richard Rossi, whose ability to gather the brightest minds in longevity science in one room has provided me with knowledge that benefits me, my family, my patients, and now you. Thanks also to Jessica Bogosian, the best veterinary technician and manager there is, and the team at Holistic Veterinary Care, who provide better care for pets than most people ever receive.

This book would not have happened without the love and support of my wife, Lee, who is unquestionably the best networker and connector of people on the planet. Without her, I would never have had the opportunity to meet the brilliant minds in science and medicine who have made me a better veterinarian. Special thanks also go to my ever-supportive and wonderful daughter, Abbey, who makes my life better every day.

ABOUT THE AUTHOR

Gary Richter, M.S., D.V.M., C.V.C., C.V.A., has been practicing veterinary medicine in the San Francisco Bay Area since 1998. In addition to conventional veterinary medical training, Dr. Richter is certified in veterinary acupuncture and veterinary chiropractic. As owner and medical director of Holistic Veterinary Care in Oakland, California, he understands the benefits of both conventional and holistic treatment methods for the preventive and the therapeutic care of pets.

Dr. Richter focuses on the integration of holistic and general-practice veterinary medicine and regenerative medicine, as well as educating professionals and pet owners on the benefits of integrative care. By combining medical cannabis with other conventional and alternative therapies, he has been able to improve the quality and quantity of life of pets living with medical conditions ranging from arthritis to inflammatory bowel disease to cancer.

The past president of the American College of Veterinary Botanical Medicine and a founding member of the Veterinary Cannabis Society, Dr. Richter has written numerous articles for print and web publications on various topics, including strategies to integrate the use of medical cannabis into conventional medical therapies for pets. His first book, *The Ultimate Pet Health Guide*, was released in 2017.

Dr. Richter's current focus is on providing information on pet health and longevity to pet owners worldwide using virtual platforms; offering highly effective, natural supplements and food for pets through his company Ultimate Pet Nutrition; and creating a wearable biometric monitor for animals through his company PetMetrics. Visit him at www.longevityforpets.com or www.ultimatepetnutrition.com.

Hay House Titles of Related Interest

YOU CAN HEAL YOUR LIFE, the movie,
starring Louise Hay & Friends
(available as an online streaming video)
www.hayhouse.com/louise-movie

THE SHIFT, the movie,
starring Dr. Wayne W. Dyer
(available as an online streaming video)
www.hayhouse.com/the-shift-movie

***

ANIMAL COMMUNICATION MADE EASY: Strengthen Your Bond and Deepen Your Connection with Animals, by Pea Horsley

ANIMAL MAGIC: The Extraordinary Proof of our Pets' Intuition and Unconditional Love for Us, by Gordon Smith

BEYOND LONGEVITY: A Proven Plan for Healing Faster, Feeling Better, and Thriving at Any Age, by Jason Prall

DOGS AND CATS HAVE SOULS TOO: Incredible True Stories of Pets Who Heal, Protect, and Communicate, by Jenny Smedley

NATURAL NUTRITION FOR CATS: The Path to Purr-fect Health, by Kymythy Schultze, C.C.N., A.H.I.

All of the above are available at your local bookstore,
or may be ordered by contacting Hay House (see next page).

***

We hope you enjoyed this Hay House book. If you'd like to receive our online catalog featuring additional information on Hay House books and products, or if you'd like to find out more about the Hay Foundation, please contact:

Hay House, Inc., P.O. Box 5100, Carlsbad, CA 92018-5100
(760) 431-7695 or (800) 654-5126
(760) 431-6948 (fax) or (800) 650-5115 (fax)
www.hayhouse.com® • www.hayfoundation.org

Published in Australia by: Hay House Australia Pty. Ltd.,
18/36 Ralph St., Alexandria NSW 2015
Phone: 612-9669-4299 • *Fax:* 612-9669-4144
www.hayhouse.com.au

Published in the United Kingdom by: Hay House UK, Ltd.,
The Sixth Floor, Watson House, 54 Baker Street, London W1U 7BU
Phone: +44 (0)20 3927 7290 • *Fax:* +44 (0)20 3927 7291
www.hayhouse.co.uk

Published in India by: Hay House Publishers India,
Muskaan Complex, Plot No. 3, B-2, Vasant Kunj, New Delhi 110 070
Phone: 91-11-4176-1620
www.hayhouse.co.in
